100

THE ROUGH GUIDE TO THE
BEST PLACES
IN THE USA

DISTRIBUTION

UK, Ireland and Europe
Apa Publications (UK) Ltd; sales@roughguides.com

United States and Canada
Ingram Publisher Services; ips@ingramcontent.com

Australia and New Zealand
Booktopia; retailer@booktopia.com.au

Worldwide
Apa Publications (UK) Ltd; sales@roughguides.com

SPECIAL SALES, CONTENT LICENSING AND CO-PUBLISHING

Rough Guides can be purchased in bulk quantities at discounted prices. We can create special editions, personalized jackets and corporate imprints tailored to your needs. Email: sales@roughguides.com
roughguides.com

HELP US UPDATE

We've gone to a lot of effort to ensure that this first edition of The Rough Guide to the 100 Best Places in the USA is accurate and up-to-date. But if you feel we've got it wrong or left something out, we'd like to know.
Please send your comments with the subject line "Rough Guides 100 Best Places in the USA" to mail@uk.roughguides.com. We'll credit all contributions and send a copy of the next edition (or any other Rough Guide if you prefer) for the very best emails.

THE ROUGH GUIDE TO THE
100 BEST PLACES IN THE USA

Editor: Zara Sekhavati

Commissioned by: Helen Fanthorpe

Picture Editor: Tom Smyth

Designer: Michal Ptasznik

Head of DTP and Pre-press: Rebeka Davies

Head of Publishing: Sarah Clark

100

THE ROUGH GUIDE TO THE
BEST PLACES IN THE USA

INTRODUCTION

Big, bright and bold, the USA has it all, from pulsating megacities to tumbleweed plains where you could hear a pin drop. This vast nation covers a land area only slightly smaller than the entire European continent, and there's extraordinary variety within its borders. From the rolling hills of New England to the scorched red canyons of the Southwest, via wide-open prairies, Great Lake shorelines and the stupendous peaks of the Rocky Mountains, nature has endowed the USA with some of the best scenery in the world. The American people – and the landmarks, towns and cities they have created – are as varied as the land they inhabit. Stetson-toting ranchers live the simple life in one-horse towns while the beautiful people sip cocktails in the rooftop bars of Brooklyn.

Let Rough Guides take you on a journey through the great U.S. of A. We've cherry-picked one hundred of the best places in the country to sate every traveller's appetite – representing destinations that are unmissable, underrated, up-and-coming or back on the tourist map. Visit carnivalesque New Orleans in the steamy south, explore the jungle-utopia of Kauai in Hawai'i, marvel at impossibly sited Ancestral Puebloan cliff dwellings in the Four Corners region or gorge on fresher-than-fresh seafood in Maine's lobster shacks. Whatever your interest, the USA has got you covered: Native American sites, revolutionary history, eclectic culture and glassy skyscrapers all rub shoulders here in the land of the free. So live like the Americans do, and start dreaming.

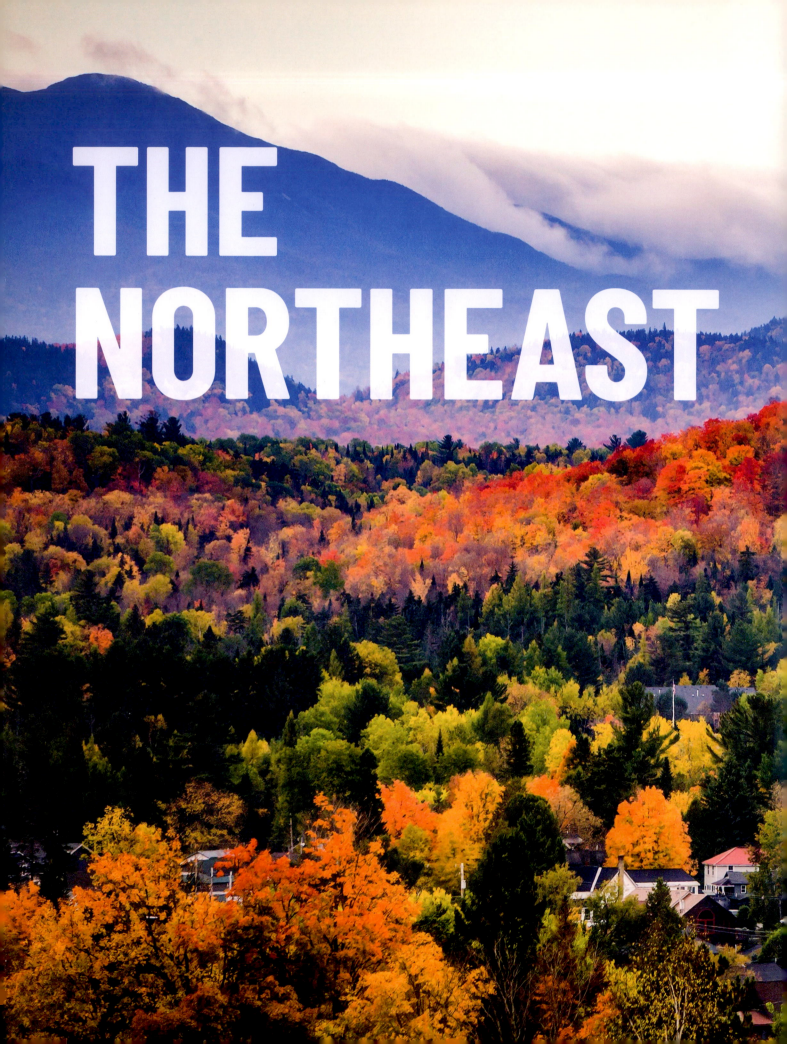

THE NORTHEAST

Sunrise from Algonquin Peak in the Adirondacks

ADIRONDACKS

NEW YORK The Adirondack Mountains, which cover an area larger than Connecticut and Rhode Island combined, are said by locals to be named after an Iroquois insult for enemies they'd driven into the forest and left to become "bark eaters". For sheer grandeur, the region is hard to beat: 46 peaks reach to more than 4000ft; in summer the purple-green mountains span far into the distance in shaggy tiers, in autumn the trees form a russet-red kaleidoscope.

Until recent decades this vast northern region between Albany and the Canadian border was almost the exclusive preserve of loggers, fur trappers and a few select New York millionaires; these days mountaineers, skiers and dedicated hikers form the majority of visitors. Outdoor pursuits are certainly the main attraction in the rugged wilderness of the Adirondacks, though a few small resorts, especially the former Winter Olympic venue of Lake Placid and its smaller neighbour Lake Saranac, offer creature comforts in addition to breaktaking scenery.

View from a fire tower over the Adirondack Mountains

Hiking on a trail through a hardwood forest in Adirondack National Park

Waterfall in the Adirondacks with autumn foliage

Ski runs on Whiteface Mountain

Back Bay and the Charles River

The Old State House

The footbridge in the Public Garden

Stores and restaurants on Newbury Street

BOSTON

MASSACHUSETTS A modern American city that trades on its colonial past, Boston is about as close to the Old World as the New World gets. Every day, hundreds of visitors walk the red line on the sidewalk that marks the 2.5-mile Freedom Trail, taking in the major sites of the city's momentous Revolutionary history. This is not to say that Boston lacks contemporary attractions: its restaurants, museums and neatly landscaped public spaces are all as alluring as its historic sites.

The city has grown up around Boston Common, a utilitarian chunk of green established for public use and "the feeding of cattell" in 1634. It's also one of the links in the string of nine parks called the Emerald Necklace; another piece is the lovely Public Garden, where Boston's iconic swan boats paddle the main pond. Grand boulevards such as Commonwealth Avenue ("Comm Ave") lead west from the Public Garden into Back Bay, where Harvard Bridge crosses into Cambridge. The beloved North End, adjacent to the waterfront, is Boston's Little Italy, its narrow streets chock-a-block with excellent bakeries and restaurants. Behind the Common rises the State House and lofty Beacon Hill, every bit as dignified as when writer Henry James called Mount Vernon Street "the most prestigious address in America".

Massachusetts Avenue in Beacon Hill

Coney Island

Street art in Bushwick

Sunbathing in Domino Park

Bedford Avenue

BROOKLYN

NEW YORK If Brooklyn were an independent city, it would be the third biggest in the USA. Across the East River from Manhattan (see page 28), this populous New York borough is where city folk spend their downtime at innovative craft breweries, subversive art galleries and performance spaces, new restaurant openings and retro bowling alleys. There's a graceful synergy between new and old Brooklyn, with its handsome brownstone townhouses, cast-iron lampposts and tree-lined streets. And although true counterculture has been pushed out to the far reaches of the borough (think Bushwick and Greenpoint), the neighbourhoods abutting waterfront DUMBO are booming. Williamsburg, too - particularly on Bedford Avenue - is a superb place to get your fill of vintage-clothing boutiques, coffee shops and record stores.

Big hitting sights in Brooklyn are not so much the point as strolling its cobblestone streets and flea markets, or soaking up the sensational Manhattan skyline from the waterfront at sunset; but Brooklyn Bridge, the Brooklyn Navy Yard and dilapidated-but-charming Coney Island are all must-sees. Foodies won't be disappointed, either: casual American-Italian, Polish, Venezuelan and Ethiopian eateries compete with upscale French brasseries and fine-dining farm-to-table fare.

CAPE MAY

NEW JERSEY Cape May was founded by the Dutch Captain Mey in 1620, on the small hook at the very southern tip of the Jersey coast. Jutting out into the Atlantic and washed by Delaware Bay on the west, the town began its days as a whaling and farming community. Tourism soon took over, aided by the town's superb beaches.

The Victorian era was Cape May's finest, when Southern plantation owners flocked to the fashionable boarding houses of this genteel "resort of Presidents". Nearly all its gingerbread architecture dates from a mass rebuilding after a severe fire in 1878. Today, the whole town is a National Historic Landmark, with more than six hundred Victorian buildings, tree-lined streets, beautifully kept gardens and a lucrative B&B industry.

Cape May's brightly coloured houses were built by nouveau riche Victorians with a healthy disrespect for subtlety. Cluttered with cupolas, gazebos, balconies and "widow's walks", the houses follow no architectural rules except excess. They were known as "patternbook homes", with designs and features chosen from catalogues and thrown together in accordance with the owner's taste.

Colourful historic Victorian houses line the waterfront in Cape May

Lookout at Mohonk Mountain House

Mohonk Mountain House resort

Belleayre Mountain ski resort slope

Farm in the Catskills

Awosting Falls in Minnewaska state park

CATSKILLS

NEW YORK You don't have to look far beyond America's biggest metropolis to find an epic wilderness to match. That's the beauty of New York State. The Catskills' 700,000 acres of forested mountain peaks protrude into the long Hudson Valley, so you're out of the Bronx and among clapboard porches between the pines in half an hour's drive. Iced with powder-snow in winter, you can ski ninety miles of slopes or snowshoe through Narnia-like backcountry. Summer brings sunny days roaming yellow- and purple-flecked meadows, hiking craggy trails to waterfall-backed swimming holes or kayaking on placid lakes.

The golden era of Catskills' resort holidays, captured in films like *Dirty Dancing*, was dwindling by the 1980s. But in the last few years, a new generation of creatives, hoteliers and restaurateurs have brought a wave of innovation upstate. Big-name chefs are relocating, inspired by the farm-to-table trend, beat-up roadside motels have been reborn with boutique flair, cocktail bars are being opened by hipster Brooklynites, small-batch beer taprooms are spreading like wildfire and the Tiny House trend has seen ingenious cabins popping up between the trees. In the Catskills' most famous small-town of Woodstock, meanwhile, legendary music hall Colony has reopened as a cornerstone of the Catskills Renaissance.

FINGER LAKES

NEW YORK Move aside Napa Valley and Sonoma: the Finger Lakes are bringing some excellent upstate wines to the table. Lesser-visited areas of New York State are often overlooked in favour of the eponymous city, but pop a cork or explore the dappled woodlands around the Finger Lakes and the crowds and crush couldn't feel further away.

Named because of the presence of eleven long, slender lakes, the region has upwards of one hundred wineries, most perched on rolling hills overlooking the waters. Along the major lakes you'll find designated wine trails; the Seneca Lake Wine Trail – tracing the largest, middle "finger" – has 35 wineries, where tastings are available against beautiful backdrops.

Towns and villages such as Ithaca, Aurora, Skaneateles, Canandaigua and Geneva have plenty of character, with excellent dining options (and craft breweries), an enviable collection of art galleries and lashings of ice cream in the summer months. Make the trip to Watkins Glen State Park, a small but impressive woodland featuring eighteen cascading waterfalls.

Watkins Glen State Park

Pier on Seneca Lake

Wine grapes in Finger Lakes

Wine glasses and Canandaigua Lake

Cannon in Gettysburg National Military Park

The Pennsylvania State Memorial

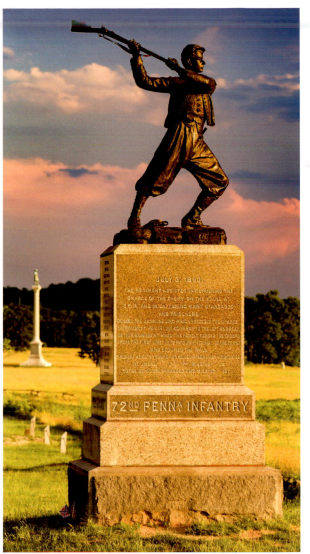

The 72nd Pennsylvania Infantry Monument

GETTYSBURG

PENNSYLVANIA Scene of one of the American Civil War's bloodiest and most decisive battles, Gettysburg thrives on its special place in the country's history books. Indeed, the small Pennsylvania college town is still surrounded by the hills of rolling grass that saw 50,000 combatants and civilians killed between July 1st and 3rd, 1863. It was here that the tide finally turned against General Robert E Lee's Confederate army and led to Abraham Lincoln's immortalized Gettysburg Address four months later.

Now punctuated by numerous silent memorials, Gettysburg National Military Park consists of areas with evocative names such as Bloody Run, Valley of Death and Cemetery Hill, attesting to the carnage that took place here.

These can be toured on your own or with a park ranger as guide. Before heading out into battlefield, it pays to take in the superb chronological account of events at the state-of-the-art Visitor Center, making sure not to miss the brilliant 360-degree cyclorama.

There are a number of other battle-related attractions here, notably the Gettysburg History Center, the Jennie Wade House and Seminary Ridge Museum, as well as the later Eisenhower National Historic Site, commemorating the President's retirement here.

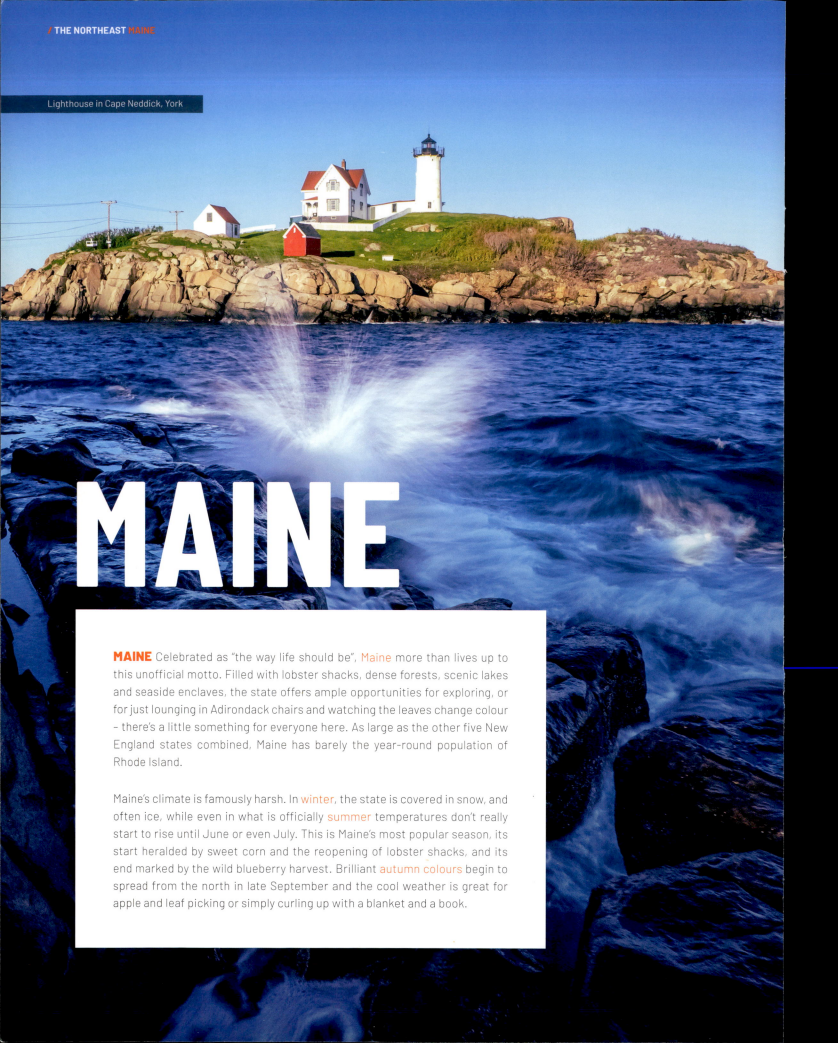

Lighthouse in Cape Neddick, York

MAINE

MAINE Celebrated as "the way life should be", Maine more than lives up to this unofficial motto. Filled with lobster shacks, dense forests, scenic lakes and seaside enclaves, the state offers ample opportunities for exploring, or for just lounging in Adirondack chairs and watching the leaves change colour – there's a little something for everyone here. As large as the other five New England states combined, Maine has barely the year-round population of Rhode Island.

Maine's climate is famously harsh. In winter, the state is covered in snow, and often ice, while even in what is officially summer temperatures don't really start to rise until June or even July. This is Maine's most popular season, its start heralded by sweet corn and the reopening of lobster shacks, and its end marked by the wild blueberry harvest. Brilliant autumn colours begin to spread from the north in late September and the cool weather is great for apple and leaf picking or simply curling up with a blanket and a book.

Blueberry barrens in East Orland

Lobster buoys for sale in Cape Neddick

Winter in Wiscasset

Trail in Acadia National Park

Manhattan skyline

Rush hour in Midtown

The High Line

The Met, the Metropolitan Museum of Art

MANHATTAN

NEW YORK Think New York City and it is Manhattan's unrivalled skyline and busy streets that spring to mind. The city's most densely populated borough stretches from Battery Park at its southern tip through the ever-evolving neighbourhoods of Lower Manhattan (the Meatpacking District, Greenwich Village and Tribeca, to name but a few), the iconic sights of Midtown and north to historic Harlem and Upper Manhattan.

Exploring The Met's immense art collection is as quintessential a New York experience as window-shopping on Fifth Avenue, taking in a Broadway show or eating bagels on the Upper West Side. At once familiar from a thousand films and TV shows and yet unlike any other city, its vibrant energy and relentless pace is intoxicating. But look further and you'll find a welcome escape in the High Line, an elevated park that runs through Chelsea – the first of its kind in the USA. Or take in the dizzying view from Edge at Hudson Yards, the highest observation deck in the Western hemisphere. Wander the undulating paths of Central Park to find street performers, free Shakespeare plays and gondolas on the lake, grab a pizza slice or drink vintage cocktails into the early hours. Everything is here.

Sunrise over Central Park and Upper East Side Manhattan

Korean War Veterans Memorial

The Lincoln Memorial

The US Capitol Building

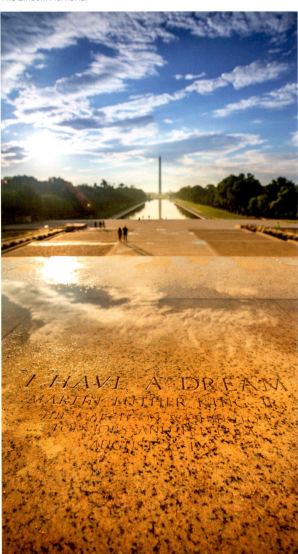

Lincoln Memorial Reflecting Pool

NATIONAL MALL

WASHINGTON DC Washington DC's National Mall, with its magnificent monuments and terrific museums, is an essential stop on any tour of the country. From the Lincoln Memorial and the White House to the US Capitol by way of the towering Washington Monument, this grand parkway is an awesome showcase of American culture and history.

The National Mall is most famous for its quartet of presidential monuments, along with the White House and the powerful memorials to veterans of the twentieth century's various wars. The elegant, two-mile-long mall is also DC's most popular green space, used for summer softball games and Fourth of July concerts. And when there's a protest gesture to be made, the Mall is the place to make it; Martin Luther King, Jr. delivered his "I Have a Dream" speech on the steps of the Lincoln Memorial. In contrast to the memorials and monuments of its western half, the National Mall's eastern side is dominated by museums, most of which are part of the spectacular Smithsonian Institution.

NIAGARA FALLS

NEW YORK Renowned as one of the planet's most iconic waterfalls, the majestic cascade of Niagara Falls straddles the border between the USA and Canada. There are in fact three distinct sections, with the taller American and Bridal Veil falls located within US territory, while the wide arc of the Horseshoe Falls connects the two countries.

Various means of viewing the gushing torrents are laid on for visitors, from the Maid of the Mist boat trip, which takes yellow waterproof-coated tourists inside the fine rainbow-creating spray, to the Cave of the Winds tour on Goat Island, which allows you behind the shimmering pane of water near its base. There is also an observation deck and expensive bird's-eye-view helicopter tours, while at night the falls are illuminated in myriad colours.

The towns on both sides of Rainbow Bridge are predictable tourist traps, but the green expanses of the national park on the American side, especially the leafy environs of Goat Island, allow you to get away from the worst of the crowds and feel more connected to the natural splendour of this unique phenomenon.

Horseshoe Falls

Valley Green Inn

VALLEY GREEN

PHILADELPHIA

PENNSYLVANIA The residents of "Philly" have much to be proud of, both on and off the field. Often overshadowed by New York and Washington DC, Philadelphia was the original capital of the nation. The Declaration of Independence and the US Constitution were both debated and signed at the Independence Hall, which houses the iconic Liberty Bell. But not all that is great about Philadelphia is more than two hundred years old. Rocky made the steps of the Philadelphia Museum of Art famous, but inside there are over 250,000 works to discover – all in a building renovated to great effect by Frank Gehry (the "Core Project" was completed in 2020).

To see a different side of Philadelphia, head along the Schuylkill river to check out the trendy neighbourhood of Manayunk. Visit the Manayunk Brewing Company to sample some local beer or get out in the open at Wissahickon Valley Park; weary walkers will want to pause for brunch at *Valley Green Inn* by the creek.

Finally, no trip to sports-mad Philly would be complete without munching on a cheesesteak and making a trip to see either the Eagles (American football), 76ers (basketball), Flyers (ice hockey), Union (association football) or the Phillies (baseball).

Pretty historic homes

The Liberty Bell

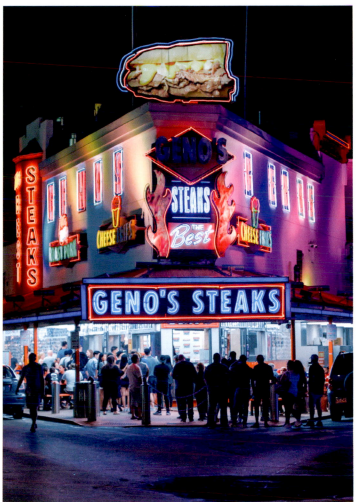

Geno's Steaks serving up its famous Philly cheesesteaks

Provincetown Carnival Parade on Commercial Street

North Provincetown Town Hall illuminated with the Pride colours

The Pilgrim Monument

Commercial Street at night

Captain Jack's Wharf

PROVINCETOWN

MASSACHUSETTS Cape Cod, on the very tip of Massachusetts, is best known as a summer seaside getaway. Yet with so many places to choose from, it's Provincetown that shouts the loudest and proudest.

P-town, as it's known amongst locals, has a lot going for it. Historically, it's where the *Mayflower* first landed in 1620 – commemorated by the Pilgrim Monument and Provincetown Museum – before moving on to Plymouth. More recently, it's a become a haven for artists and a bastion of LGBTQ culture. The friendliness, openness and drive of the community is evident everywhere, from the welcoming atmosphere to the scale and colour of the LGBTQ events hosted in this small town.

Despite its name, Commercial Street – Provincetown's main street – is captivating, offering everything from quirky coffee shops to quality seafood restaurants and sex-toy shops (hey, we said it's open). Because of its unique location, the sun here sets behind the sea – make for Race Point Beach or Herring Cove and savour the view.

Waterbury Reservoir

STOWE

VERMONT Stowe is a small town. You feel it at *Café on Main* on Main Street (where else?), where friends and neighbours greet each other over coffee, or at the weekly farmer's market, where fresh fruit pies are sold while local musicians play. It's also a town with a world-class ski resort that attracts keen skiers and snowboarders from across the world – but that doesn't detract from the charming appeal of Main Street and its mom-and-pop stores.

Follow the locals to hidden swimming holes or rent a paddle board at Waterbury Reservoir for a peaceful glide. Waterbury is also the home of the Ben & Jerry's factory – where you can indulge in an ice cream and view those varieties that never took off in the "Flavor Graveyard".

The original Von Trapps (yes, the ones who inspired *The Sound of Music*) run a hotel and craft brewery up the hill, and there are gorgeous hiking trails aplenty. Visit in September when the famous Green Mountains glow red, orange and yellow with the turning leaves, or bring your ski things and learn how to Ski the East.

Mansfield mountain ski runs

Ben and Jerry's ice cream factory

View over the town in autumn

Trapp Family Lodge

The Kancamagus Highway

Cog railway at the top of Mount Washington

Covered bridge over the Pemigewasset River on the Flume Gorge trail

A trail in a lush evergreen forest along the Kancamagus Highway

WHITE MOUNTAINS

NEW HAMPSHIRE Thanks to their accessibility from both Montréal and Boston, the enchanting White Mountains have become a year-round destination. Despite quite a lot of development flanking the main highways, the granite massifs have managed to retain their majesty. Mount Washington, at 6288ft the highest peak in the entire Northeast, claims some of the most severe weather in the world. Much of the region is protected within the White Mountains National Forest, established in 1918 and covering almost 1250 square miles today.

Piercing the range are a few high passes, called "notches", and the roads through these gaps, such as the Kancamagus Highway between Lincoln and Conway, make for enjoyably scenic routes. However, you won't really have made the most of the White Mountains unless you also set off on foot, bike or skis across the long expanses of thick evergreen forest that encircles them.

View from Cathedral Ledge at Echo Lake State Park

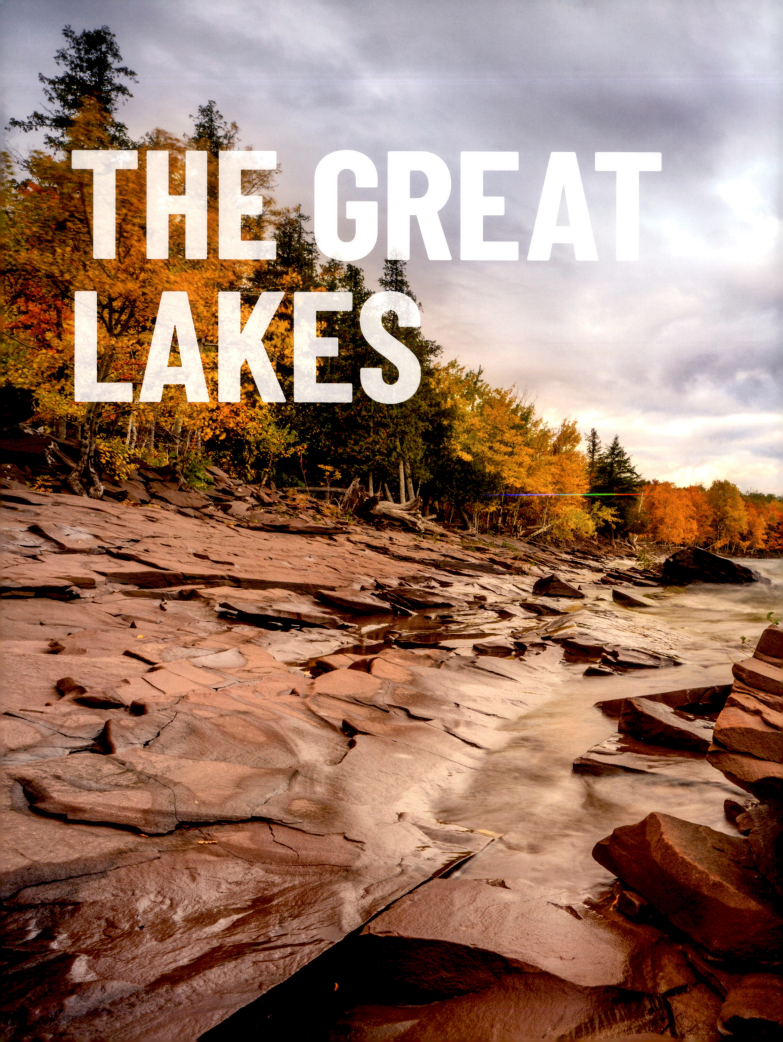

THE GREAT LAKES

Amish buggy in in Monroe County

AMISH COMMUNITIES OF WISCONSIN

WISCONSIN America's rural Midwest takes a rambling pace. Huge cow-speckled pastures front rusty-red farmhouses; come autumn, pumpkins patches sprout up between the blazing leaves. There's an old-world charm to this wholesome part of the States, especially when, as you drive along meandering roads, signs start to warn you of horses and buggies. Then, you realize the farmers are using horse-drawn ploughs on their fields. Morning worshippers are in period-drama bonnets. Living within this consumer-driven superpower of a country is a community that chooses to go back to basics: the Amish.

A Christian group with roots in Europe's sixteenth-century Protestant movement, they shun the trappings of modern life: no electricity, cars, phones, TVs or computers. Wisconsin has Amish settlements all over the state. They don't court attention, though visitors are welcome. So, pick up a driving map and peruse their shops of handcrafted furniture, quilts, rugs, baskets, home-made jam and maple syrup – cash only, of course. A tour with Down a Country Road, in Cashton, includes a personal introduction to Amish families. Spend a few hours in the company of these humble and hard-working folk, and you might take away a thing or two about the joys of embracing the simple life.

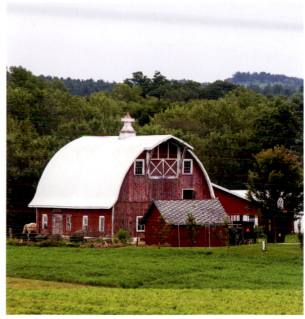

Amish farmstead in Trempealeau County

Amish boy in an old-fashioned black buggy

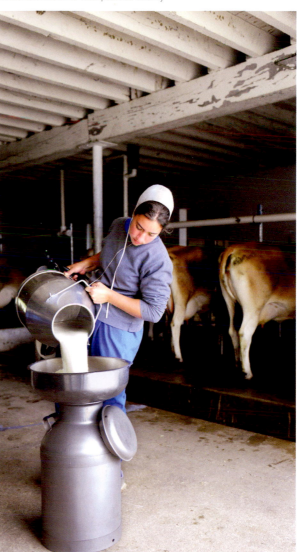

Ploughing with horses

Amish woman pouring raw milk into a filter after milking the cows

Elevated train travels on the tracks in the Loop

Chicago Theatre

Deep-dish pizza

Ferry boat passes under the DuSable Bridge over the Chicago River

CHICAGO

ILLINOIS Studded with a bewitching ensemble of skyscrapers that rise up from Lake Michigan, Chicago is one of the great American cities, forever linked with the gangsters of Al Capone, the blues of Muddy Waters and the gravity-defying dunks of Michael Jordan. Its bike-friendly layout and jaw-dropping skyline (featuring the 110-storey Willis Tower), best viewed from the boats on the Chicago River, are perhaps its most memorable features – despite some world-class museums, it's Chicago's icons and their legacies that intrigue most visitors, from the Blues Brothers to its gut-busting deep-dish pizzas.

Downtown Chicago offers a masterclass in modern architecture, with buildings that range from the prototype skyscrapers of the 1890s to Mies van der Rohe's "less is more" modernist masterpieces, and one of the tallest buildings in the world, the quarter-of-a-mile-high Willis Tower. Downtown covers several neighbourhoods and has long since expanded beyond the Loop, its traditional heart, so called because it's circled by the elevated tracks of the CTA "L" trains.

Downtown Cleveland seen from the harbour

Cleveland residential street

Exhibit at the Cleveland Museum of Art

West Side Market

CLEVELAND

OHIO Perched on the shoreline of Lake Erie in northeastern Ohio, Cleveland is part of the expansive Great Lakes region. Victorian clapboard houses line the leafy streets with the unhurriedness of small-town charm, but the city roars into action with a buzzing music scene – with the likes of the legendary Rock 'n' Roll Hall of Fame and the renowned Cleveland Orchestra – as well as homegrown chefs and their award-winning restaurants. There are plenty of heavyweight cultural attractions, too. Picks of the bunch include the Cleveland History Center, complete with an expansive automobile collection (a nod to the city's once-premier industry); the superlative Cleveland Museum of Art, displaying more than 45,000 ancient and modern works of art; and the vibrant West Side Market, where nineteenth-century immigrants once shopped for their native foods. Whether you're an art-lover, food-fanatic or you simply want to soak up the highlights, Cleveland can't be beat.

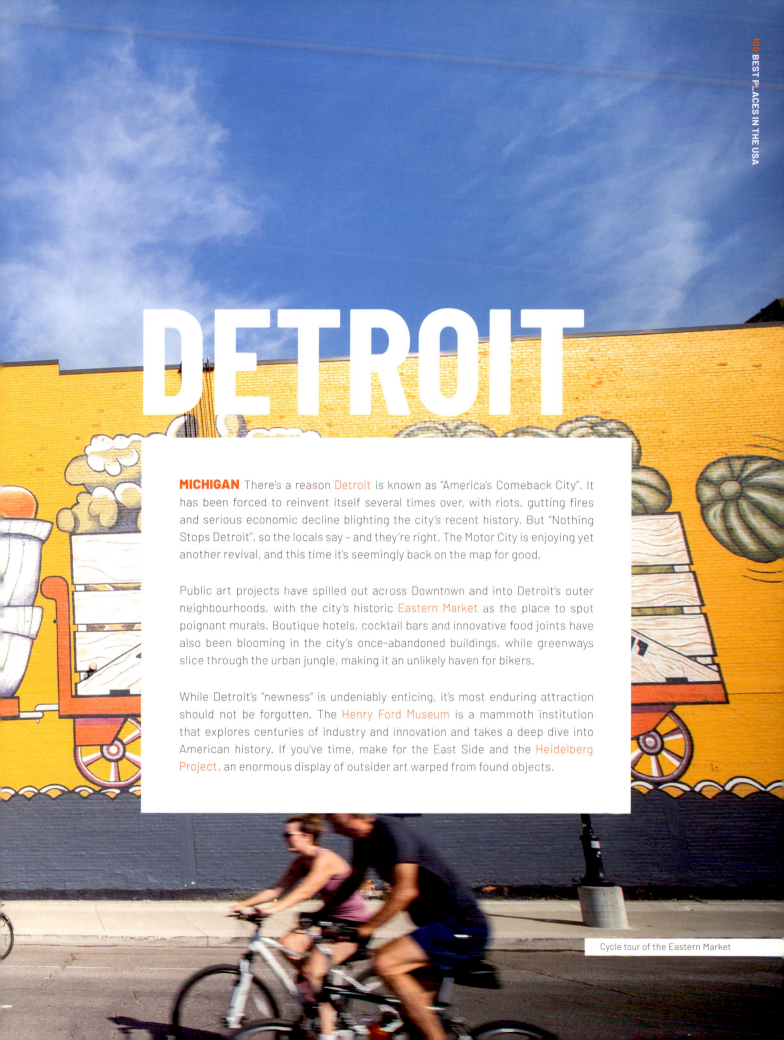

DETROIT

MICHIGAN There's a reason Detroit is known as "America's Comeback City". It has been forced to reinvent itself several times over, with riots, gutting fires and serious economic decline blighting the city's recent history. But "Nothing Stops Detroit", so the locals say – and they're right. The Motor City is enjoying yet another revival, and this time it's seemingly back on the map for good.

Public art projects have spilled out across Downtown and into Detroit's outer neighbourhoods, with the city's historic Eastern Market as the place to spot poignant murals. Boutique hotels, cocktail bars and innovative food joints have also been blooming in the city's once-abandoned buildings, while greenways slice through the urban jungle, making it an unlikely haven for bikers.

While Detroit's "newness" is undeniably enticing, it's most enduring attraction should not be forgotten. The Henry Ford Museum is a mammoth institution that explores centuries of industry and innovation and takes a deep dive into American history. If you've time, make for the East Side and the Heidelberg Project, an enormous display of outsider art warped from found objects.

Cycle tour of the Eastern Market

Local fauna

Lupine fields

INDIANA DUNES NATIONAL PARK

INDIANA Hugging more than 15 miles of the southern shore of Lake Michigan, Indiana Dunes National Park preserves giant sand dunes formed over thousands of years, as well as wetlands, prairies, meandering rivers and tranquil pine forests. The park is also a rich habitat for rare bird species, and is laced with over 50 miles of trails.

The park coastline is sprinkled with fine beaches, with Central Avenue Beach an especially narrow strip backed by sandy cliffs, and Mount Baldy Beach dominated by a 126ft-high sand dune. The Portage Lakefront and Riverwalk is an ideal spot to watch for migrating birds in the spring and summer. Behind Dunbar Beach dunes lies the Great Marsh, a large inter-dunal wetland. Flocks of coots, mallards, and wood ducks glide over the wetlands, while green herons stalk and beavers play in the channels. From Dunbar Beach, the Dunes Ridge Trail provides panoramic views of the marshes.

Further inland, trails follow the serene Little Calumet River through forests of maple, beech, basswood and oak, and across the recently restored Mnoké Prairie for a glimpse of the once vast pre-settlement grasslands. Wildflowers speckle the trails along the river in spring.

Boardwalks zigzag the sand dunes

Chippewa Harbor, Isle Royale

ISLE ROYALE NATIONAL PARK

MICHIGAN The 45-mile sliver of Isle Royale National Park, fifty miles out in Lake Superior, is geographically and culturally very, very far from urban America. All cars are banned on this blissfully undeveloped enclave, and instead of freeways, 166 miles of hiking trails lead past windswept trees, swampy lakes, paddling loons and grazing moose. The only traces of human life here are ancient mineworks, possibly two millennia old, shacks left behind by commercial fishermen in the 1940s, and a few lighthouses and park buildings. Hiking, canoeing, fishing and scuba-diving among shipwrecks are the principal leisure activities.

Two small visitor centres operate on the island itself, at Rock Harbor and at Windigo, usually open July and August only. Rock Harbor sits at the northeast end of the island, surrounded by forests of spruce, birch and fir. Out in the harbour is tiny Raspberry Island, laced with planked trails through the woods and bogs here, home to the rare insect-eating sundew and pitcher plants. Windigo lies on the southwest coast of Isle Royale, at the end of secluded Washington Harbor. From here trails also fan out through the boreal forest and hills, while crested merganser ducks, otters and moose all reside in and around the water.

Rock Harbor Lighthouse

Beaver swimming on Isle Royale

Moskey Basin

Snowshoe hare

PICTURED ROCKS NATIONAL LAKESHORE

MICHIGAN Covering a 42-mile stretch of Lake Superior, the Pictured Rocks National Lakeshore offers a splendid array of multicoloured cliffs, rolling dunes and secluded sandy beaches. Over the millennia rain, wind, ice and sun have carved and gouged the arches, columns and caves into the face of the lakeshore, all stained different hues. The best way to see the cliffs is by boat. Hwy-58 runs along the edge of the park from the small village of Grand Marais to Munising, but there are only a few sights on route, notably the Log Slide (a large dune) and Miners Castle, a jagged column of rock twelve miles east of Munising. With more time it's worth hiking the trails that run from Hwy-58 out to the shoreline, notably the fine loop to Chapel Falls and Chapel Beach.

Kayak tour of a sea cave under Miners Castle

Coastline at Pictured Rocks National Lakeshore

Grand Island East Channel Lighthouse

Lovers Leap

Roots stretch across a chasm from the mainland to Chapel Rock

Gallery tour

Artist at the Sharon Weiss Gallery

Columbus skyline from Bicentennial Park

Mural in the Short North Arts District

SHORT NORTH ARTS DISTRICT

OHIO Ohio's state capital and home to the massive Ohio State University, Columbus is a likeable place to visit. At the top end of downtown is Short North Arts District, a former red-light district that's now the city's most vibrant enclave. Standing on either side of High Street – the main north–south thoroughfare – its entrance is marked by the iron gateways of the Cap at Union Station. Thereafter starts the trail of galleries, bars and restaurants that makes the area so popular with locals; it is also the heart of the LGBTQ community. The first Saturday of each month sees the Gallery Hop, when local art-dealers throw open their doors – complementing the artworks with wine, snacks and occasional performance pieces – and the socializing goes on well into the evening.

View down High Street in Short North Arts District

Lincoln Home National Historic Site

The dome in the Illinois State Capitol building

Display at the Abraham Lincoln Presidential Library and Museum

The Cozy Dog Drive In restaurant

SPRINGFIELD

ILLINOIS In an age of increased political polarization, comforting memories of Abraham Lincoln envelope the Illinois state capital of Springfield, where the man consistently voted the greatest US president lived for a large part of his life. His shadow looms large at the Lincoln Home National Historic Site, the Lincoln Tomb and the Abraham Lincoln Presidential Library and Museum.

Elsewhere, history aficionados are lured from Route 66 (it passes right through the town) by the impressive 116-year-old Dana-Thomas House: a Frank Lloyd Wright-designed masterwork of angular, elegant beauty. Such heavyweight tourist draws aren't typical of a US settlement of just 113,000 – and yet it's the small-town charm that provides Springfield's greatest appeal.

To explore the manicured lawns and botanical gardens of Washington Park, before admiring the smart, sturdy Illinois State Capitol building, feels surreally familiar – like stepping onto the set of a US TV show. Enjoy a milkshake at *Charlie Parker's Diner* before catching a movie at the Route 66 Drive In Theater for peak Americana.

TALIESIN

WISCONSIN Frank Lloyd Wright's final home and one of his masterpieces, Taliesin is a pricey but essential highlight for fans of architecture or American history. The 600-acre estate comprises five Lloyd Wright structures, the most important of which is Taliesin itself, completed in 1911 and a stunning example of the Prairie School. Many of Wright's most famous buildings were designed in the studio here (including the Guggenheim Museum). Nearby, the Hillside Home School was completed by Wright in 1902, also in the Prairie School style, and today remains a prestigious postgraduate college for architects.

Tours add context to the architecture but also the traumatic events that took place here. Lloyd Wright left Chicago in 1909, abandoning his family for his mistress Mamah Cheney. They eventually moved to the Wisconsin River valley, near to where Lloyd Wright was born; he named his new home Taliesin in homage to his Welsh roots. Tragically, Mamah was murdered at the house by a deranged servant in 1914 (along with her two children, and four others), and the house was burned down. A heartbroken Wright rebuilt, but the house burned again in 1925 (this time by accident). He again rebuilt, "Taliesin III" remaining his primary residence until he died in 1959.

Taliesin in winter

THE PLAINS

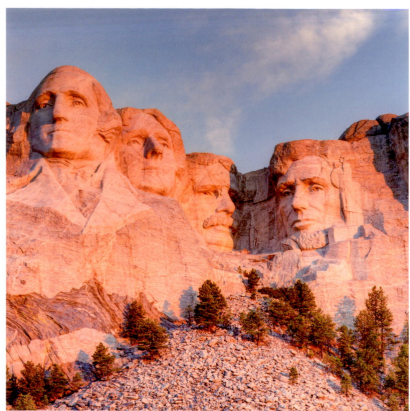
Mount Rushmore

Prairie dogs

/ Crazy Horse Memorial

Striking granite formations in the Black Hills

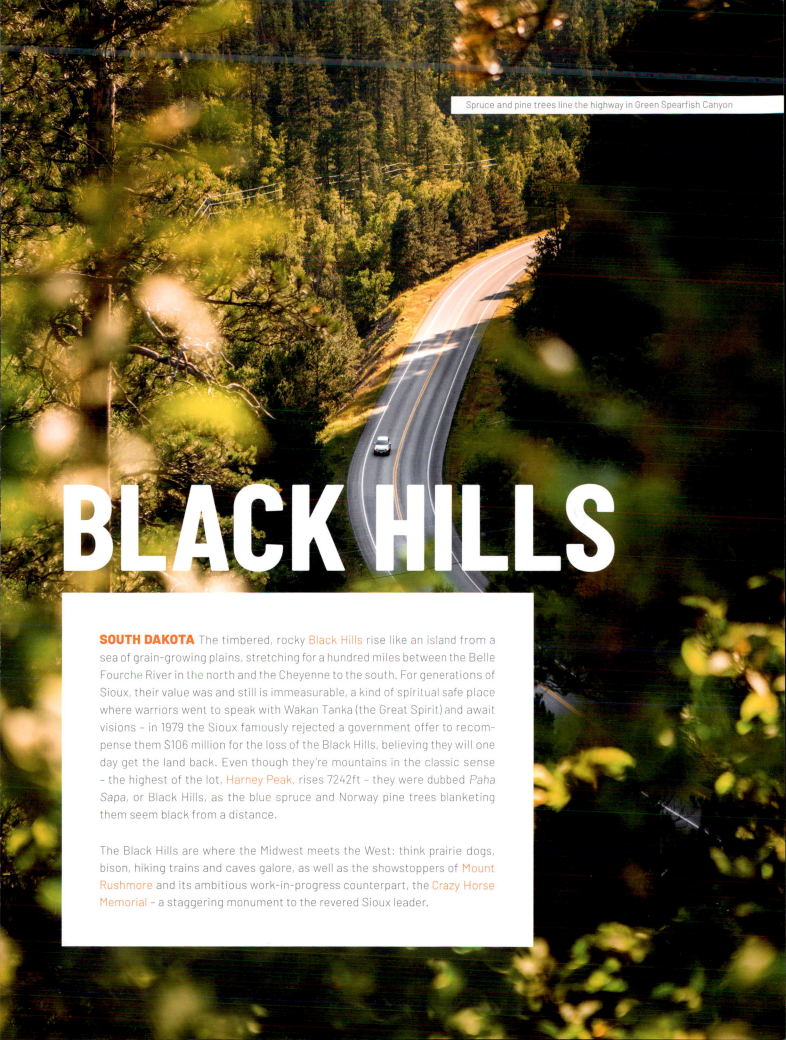

BLACK HILLS

SOUTH DAKOTA The timbered, rocky Black Hills rise like an island from a sea of grain-growing plains, stretching for a hundred miles between the Belle Fourche River in the north and the Cheyenne to the south. For generations of Sioux, their value was and still is immeasurable, a kind of spiritual safe place where warriors went to speak with Wakan Tanka (the Great Spirit) and await visions – in 1979 the Sioux famously rejected a government offer to recompense them $106 million for the loss of the Black Hills, believing they will one day get the land back. Even though they're mountains in the classic sense – the highest of the lot, Harney Peak, rises 7242ft – they were dubbed *Paha Sapa*, or Black Hills, as the blue spruce and Norway pine trees blanketing them seem black from a distance.

The Black Hills are where the Midwest meets the West: think prairie dogs, bison, hiking trains and caves galore, as well as the showstoppers of Mount Rushmore and its ambitious work-in-progress counterpart, the Crazy Horse Memorial – a staggering monument to the revered Sioux leader.

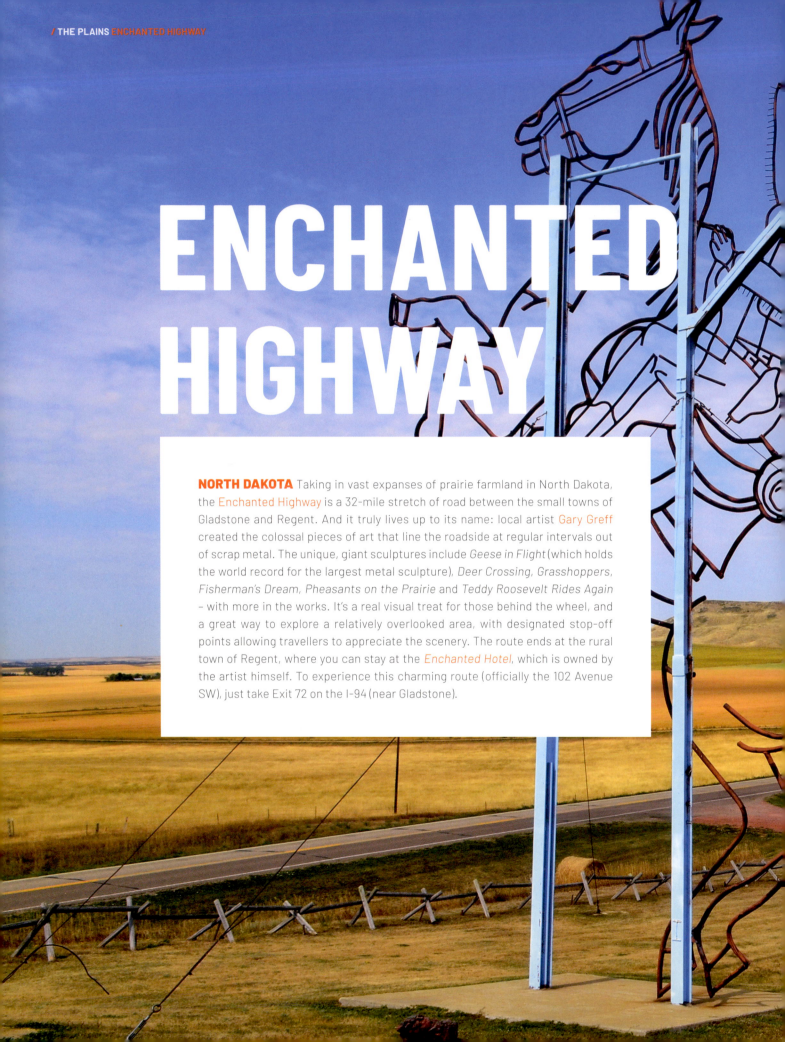

ENCHANTED HIGHWAY

NORTH DAKOTA Taking in vast expanses of prairie farmland in North Dakota, the Enchanted Highway is a 32-mile stretch of road between the small towns of Gladstone and Regent. And it truly lives up to its name: local artist Gary Greff created the colossal pieces of art that line the roadside at regular intervals out of scrap metal. The unique, giant sculptures include *Geese in Flight* (which holds the world record for the largest metal sculpture), *Deer Crossing*, *Grasshoppers*, *Fisherman's Dream*, *Pheasants on the Prairie* and *Teddy Roosevelt Rides Again* – with more in the works. It's a real visual treat for those behind the wheel, and a great way to explore a relatively overlooked area, with designated stop-off points allowing travellers to appreciate the scenery. The route ends at the rural town of Regent, where you can stay at the *Enchanted Hotel*, which is owned by the artist himself. To experience this charming route (officially the 102 Avenue SW), just take Exit 72 on the I-94 (near Gladstone).

Teddy Roosevelt Rides Again on the Enchanted Highway

Horse and tallgrass in Flint Hills

Flint Hills National Scenic Byway

Hays House Restaurant

Trail in the Tallgrass Prairie National Preserve

FLINT HILLS NATIONAL SCENIC BYWAY

KANSAS Rolling hills and breathtaking sunsets characterize the Flint Hills National Scenic Byway. This awe-inspiring route stretches 47.2 miles between Council Grove and Cassoday in east-central Kansas, through the largest remaining expanse of tallgrass prairie in North America. Those who hit the road will come by cattle ranches, iconic nineteenth-century limestone buildings, quirky art galleries and stunning vistas that have remained unchanged for thousands of years.

A variety of people and wildlife call the Flint Hills home. The tallgrass ecosystem is one of the most biodiverse on Earth, supporting as many as six hundred plant species and 1500 different insects. The landscape is dotted with cows, making it easy to imagine the Kaw and Osage tribes hunting wild buffalo, as they did when they lived on these plains.

Highlights along the way include the historic Hays House Restaurant (they do a seriously good strawberry pie), the Tallgrass Prairie National Preserve, with its limestone mansion and Cottonwood Falls, where you can tour the Chase County Courthouse and the Old Cowboy Jail. Perhaps best of all, be sure to stop at the Scenic Byway Overlook for an unparalleled 360-degree view across the prairie.

A.D. [J] 1881

The limestone Jones ranch house, Tallgrass Prairie National Preserve

The Old Courthouse

Aerial view of the Gateway Arch entrance

Getting up close at Gateway Arch

The glittering gateway

GATEWAY ARCH NATIONAL PARK

MISSOURI An astonishing feat of engineering, the Gateway Arch dominates Downtown St Louis; a glittering arc of steel, its vast size is hard to appreciate until you get up close. Designed by Finnish-born architect Eero Saarinen and completed in 1965, the 630ft-high stainless-steel parabola commemorates the role of St Louis in the western expansion of the USA, especially honouring the epic Lewis and Clark Expedition, which set off from here in 1804.

The four-minute "Tram Ride to the Top" shoots up the hollow, gently curving arch to the Observation Deck, where the views of St Louis, the mighty Mississippi and the surrounding tree-studded plains are spectacular. Below the arch lies the interactive Museum at the Gateway Arch, with six themed galleries spanning the history of St Louis and westward expansion from 1764 to 1965. The adjacent Tucker Theater screens the enlightening *Monument to the Dream* documentary movie, while one-hour Mississippi cruises aboard replica paddlewheelers depart from the levee below the Arch.

The Sower on top of the Nebraska State Capitol

NEBRASKA STATE CAPITOL

NEBRASKA Soaring above the plains like a fantastical, Byzantine skyscraper, this has to be one of America's most enthralling capitol buildings. Dwarfing the rest of downtown, the Art Deco tower of the 1932-built Nebraska State Capitol protrudes a staggering 400ft into the skyline. The "Tower of the Plains" is topped by a golden dome and a statue of a seed sower on a pedestal of wheat and corn, but the interior is just as awe-inspiring. The lofty mural-smothered vestibule and rotunda are as grand as a cathedral, while the unicameral chamber has a gold-stencilled ceiling. Take the elevator up to the fourteenth-floor observation deck for a bird's eye view of Nebraska's dynamic capital city, Lincoln, spread out below.

Nebraska's Supreme Court chamber

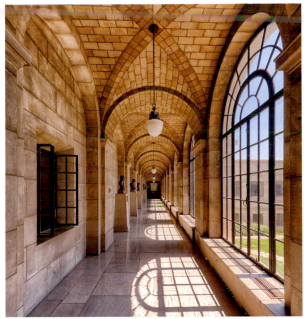

Statue-lined corridor

East Chamber

Exterior view of Nebraska State Capitol

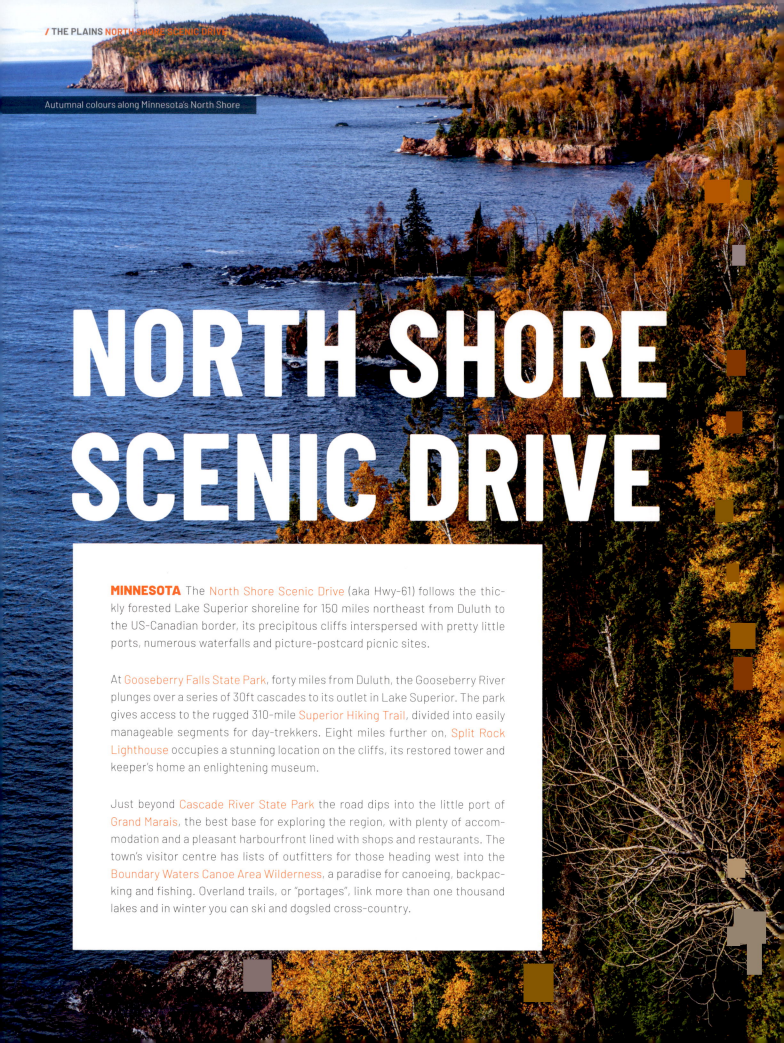

Autumnal colours along Minnesota's North Shore

NORTH SHORE SCENIC DRIVE

MINNESOTA The North Shore Scenic Drive (aka Hwy-61) follows the thickly forested Lake Superior shoreline for 150 miles northeast from Duluth to the US-Canadian border, its precipitous cliffs interspersed with pretty little ports, numerous waterfalls and picture-postcard picnic sites.

At Gooseberry Falls State Park, forty miles from Duluth, the Gooseberry River plunges over a series of 30ft cascades to its outlet in Lake Superior. The park gives access to the rugged 310-mile Superior Hiking Trail, divided into easily manageable segments for day-trekkers. Eight miles further on, Split Rock Lighthouse occupies a stunning location on the cliffs, its restored tower and keeper's home an enlightening museum.

Just beyond Cascade River State Park the road dips into the little port of Grand Marais, the best base for exploring the region, with plenty of accommodation and a pleasant harbourfront lined with shops and restaurants. The town's visitor centre has lists of outfitters for those heading west into the Boundary Waters Canoe Area Wilderness, a paradise for canoeing, backpacking and fishing. Overland trails, or "portages", link more than one thousand lakes and in winter you can ski and dogsled cross-country.

A hiking trail in Gooseberry Falls State Park

Cross Bay Lake in the Boundary Waters Canoe Area Wilderness

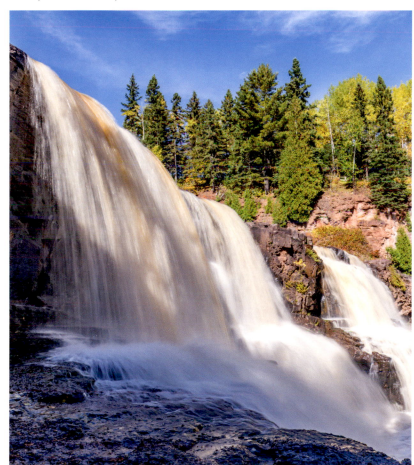

Gooseberry River cascades

Split Rock Lighthouse in winter

As Long as the Waters Flow, a statue of a Native American woman outside the Oklahoma State Capitol

Cherokee National Homecoming parade, Tahlequah

Colourful retro Phillips 66 gas station, Cushing

Buck Atom's Cosmic Curios on 66 store, Tulsa

OKLAHOMA

OKLAHOMA Wedged between Texas to the south and Kansas to the north, Oklahoma is more West than Midwest, where ranchers sport Stetsons, Native American tribes mingle with oilmen and locals say "fixin' to" a whole lot. Created in 1907 and romanticized by Rogers & Hammerstein in their first musical, *Oklahoma!*, the state was one of the hardest hit by the Depression in the 1930s, encapsulated most famously in John Steinbeck's novel *The Grapes of Wrath*, but also in Dorothea Lange's haunting photographs and in the sad yet hopeful songs of local boy Woody Guthrie. Today the state is a solidly Republican, conservative stronghold, the "buckle" of the Bible Belt.

For visitors the main draws are Americana-laced Route 66, great live music and a couple of dynamic cities; artsy Tulsa, in the hilly and wooded northeast, and the revitalized capital, Oklahoma City. The state also claims a large Native American population with 39 sovereign tribes – "Oklahoma" is a Choctaw word for "red man" – and many of its towns host museums devoted to Native American history.

Tulsa

Cannonball concretions

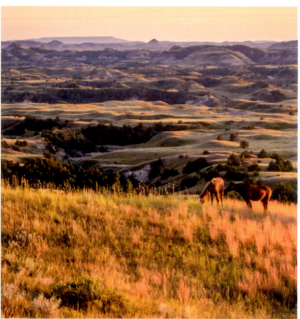

The view over the park from Juniper Campground

/ Theodore Roosevelt's Maltese Cross Cabin

Prairie dog

THEODORE ROOSEVELT NATIONAL PARK

NORTH DAKOTA A vast tract of multihued rock formations, rough grassland and badlands, Theodore Roosevelt National Park is North Dakota's unspoiled wilderness, named after the adventurer and future president who roamed, hunted and ranched here in the 1880s. Split into North and South units along the banks of the Little Missouri River, approximately 70 miles apart, the park is at its most beautiful at sunrise or sundown – the best times to observe mule deer, wild horses, elk, pronghorn, ever-present bison and closely knit prairie-dog communities.

At the main entrance to the park, the Medora Visitor Center contains a small museum dedicated to Theodore Roosevelt; behind it sits the simple Maltese Cross Cabin that served as Roosevelt's first home in North Dakota in 1884. The jaw-dropping Painted Canyon, also in the South Unit, is another highlight.

The park's smaller North Unit receives only a fraction of the visitors of its counterpart, though it's arguably more spectacular. There are staggering views from River Bend Outlook, a stunning 14-mile scenic drive and similar vistas from Oxbow Outlook, while the demanding 12-mile Buckhorn Trail winds through sage-filled terrain before following steep gulches up into lofty prairies full of gazing bison.

Wandering grouse

Ellsworth Rock Gardens

Lake Kabetogama

Boardwalk between Rainy Lake and Kettle Falls Hotel

VOYAGEURS NATIONAL PARK

MINNESOTA Set along the border between Minnesota and Canada, Voyageurs National Park is a dazzling maze of interconnected lakes and water highways – naturally best explored by boat. Once out on the lakes, you're in a great, silent world. Kingfishers, osprey and eagles swoop down for walleye; moose and bear stalk the banks.

Cruises depart the Kabetogama and Rainy Lake visitor centres, while during freeze-up – usually from December until March – the park becomes a prime destination for skiers and snowmobilers. Highlights include the white granite cliffs of Anderson Bay, providing sensational views across Rainy Lake, and the similarly vertiginous bluffs of Grassy Bay, rising some 125ft (38m) above Sand Point Lake.

On the northern shore of Lake Kabetogama, Jack Ellsworth began the Ellsworth Rock Gardens in the 1940s, using the natural Minnesota landscape to create unique sculptures and flower terraces backed by dense forest. To the southeast, the shores of Hoist Bay preserve relics from early twentieth-century logging camps, and resorts of the 1930s. Right on the Canadian border and only accessible by boat or float plane, historic *Kettle Falls Hotel* was built between 1910 and 1913, when construction of the adjacent Kettle Falls dam began – today it's the only lodging within the park.

Canoeing in Voyageurs National Park

WICHITA

KANSAS Thanks to the *Wizard of Oz*, most people have heard of Kansas even if they have very little idea of what it's like beyond the movies: vast fields of corn, twisters, *Little House on the Prairie* and the boyhood home of Clark Kent (aka Superman). The largest city in Kansas is Wichita, a cowboy town with a remarkable tradition of popular culture icons, from the *Dennis the Menace* cartoon strip (the US version is set in Wichita) and Pizza Hut (founded here in 1958), to key members of the 1950s Beat Movement (Allen Ginsberg wrote *Wichita Vortex Sutra* after he visited in 1966, to "see where everyone came from") and influential local billionaires the Koch brothers, the conservative activists Democrats love to hate. It can be hard to absorb all this bewildering heritage on a single visit, but Wichita has an intriguing range of museums and galleries, nonetheless. Standouts include the fascinating Kansas African American Museum, the Old Cowtown Museum and the Wichita Art Museum, which includes a good selection of American Impressionism.

Cattle drive at the Old Cowtown Museum

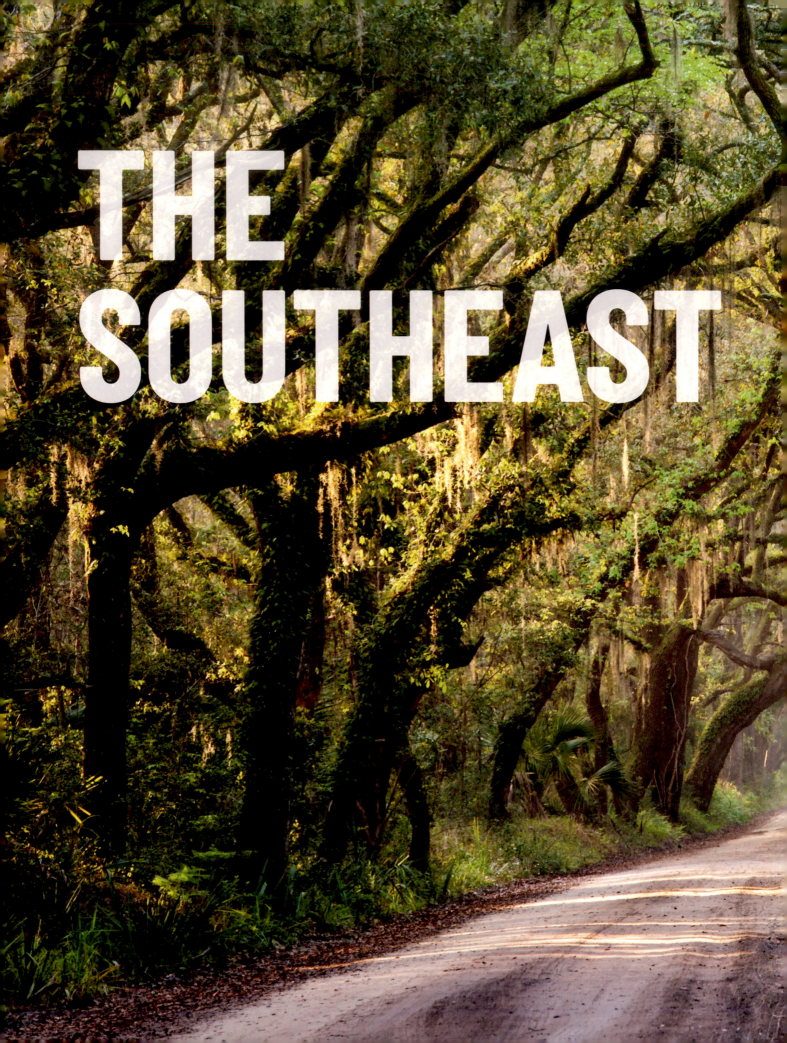

THE SOUTHEAST

CHARLESTON

SOUTH CAROLINA It's easy to fall for the old-world charms of this southern belle: quaint cobbled streets, grand antebellum mansions, horse-drawn carriages and southern hospitality. But the South Carolina city of Charleston is not just about genteel sophistication. This is a place with an edgy vibe, a thriving cultural life and a flourishing food and bar scene.

Founded 350 years ago by English colonists, the settlement was named Charles Town after King Charles II. Built through slave labour, the city became hugely prosperous from rice and cotton cultivation. A stroll along the quiet leafy streets will reveal meticulously restored houses of peeling, multicoloured stucco and wooden shutters, many once owned by plantation owners, some now preserved as museums. History is palpable at the Old Exchange and Provost Dungeon, where Revolutionary prisoners were held, the Old Slave Mart Museum, with its harrowing story of the slave trade, and Fort Sumter, where the first shots of the Civil War were fired. No visit is complete without a tour of one of the Charleston plantations, across the Ashley River, to see the historic houses with their glorious gardens and live oaks, draped in Spanish moss.

With so much to see, it's not surprising that tourism is thriving here. As the locals say, "y'all come visit".

Historic homes in Charleston

CLARKSDALE

MISSISSIPPI The blues were born in the Mississippi Delta, where funky little Clarksdale is the obvious first port of call. The most significant town south of Memphis (see page 110), Clarksdale has an irresistible appeal and the unquestionable right to claim itself as the home of the blues. It has a phenomenal roll call of former residents, stretching from Son House, Muddy Waters, John Lee Hooker, Howlin' Wolf and Robert Johnson up to Ike Turner and Sam Cooke.

Clarksdale's music festivals are a major draw, among them the free Sunflower River Blues & Gospel Festival in August, and the Juke Joint Festival in April. Some seventy miles south of Clarksdale, down-at-heel Greenville, the largest town on the Delta and an important riverport, hosts the Mississippi Delta Blues & Heritage Festival in mid-September.

Terry "Harmonica" Bean performs at the Club Red jazz club

The Hopson Plantation's converted commissary building, now a jazz venue and bar

Deak's Mississippi Saxophone and Blues Emporium

Mural of Mississippi jazz musician Robert Johnson in Clarksdale

The James Craig Jewellers shop on Duke of Gloucester Street

A Fife-and-Drum Corps marches in Williamsburg

A horse-drawn carriage awaits

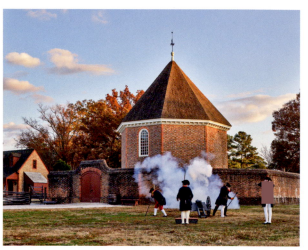

The powder magazine

COLONIAL WILLIAMSBURG HISTORIC AREA

VIRGINIA The splendid recreation of Colonial Williamsburg is an essential tourist experience for anyone with a bent for American history. While you have to buy a pricey ticket to look inside the restored buildings, the grounds are open all the time, and you can wander freely down the cobblestone streets and across the green commons.

From the Wren Building on the William and Mary campus, separated from Colonial Williamsburg by a mock-historic shopping centre, Duke of Gloucester Street runs east through the historic area to the old Capitol. The first of its eighteenth-century buildings is the Episcopalian Bruton Parish Church, where all the big names of the Revolutionary period were known to visit, and which has served as a house of worship for nearly three hundred years. Behind the church, the broad Palace Green spreads north to the Governor's Palace. West of the church, the 1771 courthouse and the octagonal powder magazine, protected by a guardhouse, face each other in the midst of Market Square. Further along, Chowning's Tavern, a reconstruction of an alehouse that stood here in 1766, is a functioning pub with lively entertainment.

A horse-drawn carriage carrying visitors

Christ of the Ozarks statue

EUREKA SPRINGS

ARKANSAS Nestled in the Ozark Mountains, not quite on or off the tourist map, Eureka Springs enjoys that rare combination of well-preserved natural beauty and easy access – albeit by car. Approaching from the south, along the ridge crest traced by Route 62, you'll see from up high how Eureka Springs clings to both sides of the steep, narrow valley. Every tree, street, hotel, spa and house clamours for access to one of the 140 cold-water springs, renowned for their healing powers.

Victorian architecture arrived here with a vengeance in the 1800s and it never went out of fashion. The style can be seen in nearly all of the city's buildings, cut from local stone and built along five winding and mountainous miles of streets, steps and walkways. A rare architectural exception is the 65ft-tall Christ of the Ozarks statue, erected on Magnetic Mountain in a somewhat bizarre bid to recreate Jerusalem. The project flopped, but it paved the way for the nearby Thorncrown Chapel, an extraordinary woodland construction of skylights and indigenous wood beams.

The valley levels out at the massive spring-fed Lake Leatherwood – man made but beautiful nonetheless, with views reminiscent of Lake Como.

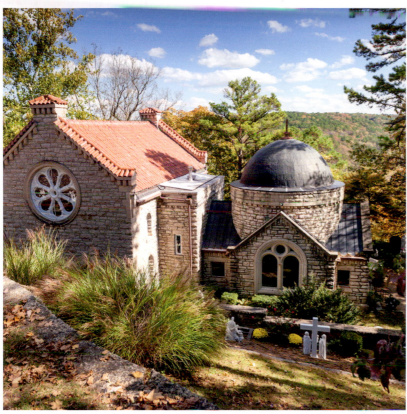

St. Elizabeth Catholic Church and the valley

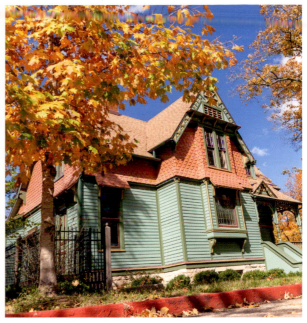

Victorian house

Historic Downtown

Thorncrown Chapel

Young gator

Hiking in the park

Airboat tour

Great white egret

EVERGLADES NATIONAL PARK

FLORIDA Florida's vast, watery wilderness, the Everglades has a raw but subtle appeal that makes a stark contrast to America's more rugged national parks. The most dramatic sights are small pockets of trees poking above a completely flat sawgrass plain, yet these wide-open spaces resonate with life, forming part of an ever-changing ecosystem. The sawgrass is replenished by water that flows as a wide sheet from Lake Okeechobee to the coast, sustaining a food chain that ends with larger wildlife such as alligators. Where natural indentations in the limestone fill with marl, tree islands – or "hammocks" – appear. Close to hammocks, often surrounding gator holes, are wispy green-leafed willows, pinewoods and, in the deep depressions that hold water the longest, dwarf cypress trees, their treetops forming a distinctive "cypress dome".

Cypress trees in the Everglades

House in the Historic District of Key West

Highway 1 to Key West in the Florida Keys

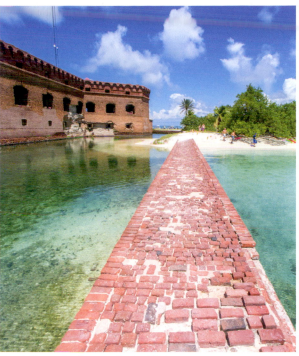
Fort Jefferson, Dry Tortugas National Park

Sloppy Joe's Bar on Duval Street

Smathers Beach, Key West

FLORIDA KEYS

FLORIDA The Florida Keys make for a steamy subtropical destination, closer to Cuba than Orlando. Best known for deep-sea fishing and the Florida Reef – the only living coral barrier reef in the USA – this southern string of islands is connected to the mainland by a 113-mile-long highway, which navigates a scenic ocean route across 42 bridges. The end of the road is historic Key West, the laidback island-city which so captivated writer Ernest Hemingway. A one-time reputation for prohibition-era speakeasies lives on today in the bars along Duval Street, and during the nightly sunset celebration on Mallory Square.

Don't miss an outing to the white-sand beach-fringed Dry Tortugas, 67 miles off the coast of Key West. Getting here by seaplane is something else – turtles, sharks and shipwrecks are spotted as you fly low over the green-blue water.

Casablanca Cafe

A Sun Trolley takes visitors around

Stonewall National Museum & Archives

A monthly Sunday jazz brunch takes place at Riverwalk

FORT LAUDERDALE

FLORIDA If the Sunshine State's a family of colourful, charismatic destinations all scrambling for attention, Fort Lauderdale's the cool, big-brother city that doesn't need to brag. It has the tropical good-time vibes of Key West, but without the remoteness; the luxury resorts of Palm Beach, but without the ostentation. It also has all the big-city conveniences of nearby Miami – but at around two-fifths the size, it's far more accessible. Meanwhile, 165 miles of waterways lend the "Venice of America" a sparkly sophistication all of its own.

Boasting seven miles of blissful beaches, this smart city has hosted many a sunset-destination wedding and as many honeymooners – among them, many same-sex couples. Indeed, Fort Lauderdale's an LGBTQ-friendly paradise – best exemplified by the buzzing gaybourhood of Wilton Manors – thanks in part to the increased targeted-marketing spend of the Greater Fort Lauderdale Convention & Visitors Bureau in recent years, including its support of the Southern Comfort Transgender Conference since 2017. That said, important LGBTQ cultural and historical spaces such as the Stonewall National Museum & Archives and the World AIDS Museum are essential stop offs no matter your sexuality or gender identity.

Sunrise over Great Smoky Mountains

GREAT SMOKY MOUNTAINS

TENNESSEE After a long day, the trees of the Great Smoky Mountains, or "the Smokies" as they're affectionately known, exude a blue haze that rises like a spectral net and gives the mountain range its name. Indeed, "shaconage", the Cherokee name for this area, means "land of blue smoke".

As you climb through the hills, the trees take on a different shade of brilliant green and you're likely to find a spongy moss underfoot that gives the impression of walking on a cloud. Gushing creeks, lush fields and thick canopies of trees furnish the land, and you can go wild swimming in waterfalls, watch the sun set behind the mountains or simply bask in all the bewitching natural beauty. Look out for bears, too – the Smokies lay claim to the densest black bear population in the Eastern United States. The mountains are also home to a host of other critters, including butterflies, salamanders and snakes.

And if all those stupendous views start to blur into one, there's always Dollywood to entertain the restless: a theme park dedicated entirely to Dolly Parton, where you can find all the usual rides and rollercoasters, as well as by one of the world's last working steam trains.

Mountain stream with autumnal colours

Chimney Tops Trail

Black bear foraging in the forest

A stunning view over the Great Smoky Mountains

Enjoying alfresco dining and drinking

Alpine architecture

Tubing along the Chattahoochee River

Shopping in downtown

HELEN

GEORGIA The scent of cinnamon wafts through the thin mountain air in Helen, a small Appalachian town in northeastern Georgia, as fennel cake is deep fried and sprinkled with powdered spices, while log smoke puffs from the chimneys of its Bavarian-style buildings. When the logging industry – and town – slid into decline in the mid-twentieth century, innovative locals began a successful rebrand, remodelling Helen on a Germanic Alpine settlement. Today, white-plaster facades, separated by timber beams and topped with red turreted roofs, line Main Street, housing beer halls, souvenir shops and fudgeries. Christmas lights sparkle in the dark winter months, strung from festive market stalls erected in the open square around a towering Christmas tree. In summer, visitors can take part in a range of all-American activities including fishing, hiking, wine-tasting and even gold panning. Tubing down the Chattahoochee River, meanwhile, is a rite of passage; grab a large fluro-coloured rubber ring and float through fairy-tale woodland landscapes and into town, passing outdoor decks where revellers cheers their beers at tubers as they drift by. *Prost!*

Helen's main square

LOUISVILLE

KENTUCKY Located on the south bank of the mighty Ohio River, with views across to the Falls of the Ohio, Louisville is famous for three main reasons: the Kentucky Derby, bourbon and Muhammad Ali. Apart from the hordes that flock here for America's most famous horse race every May, the city has a growing reputation for arts and festivals, as well as the hip bar scene along Bardstown Road. Somewhat surprisingly, the area around Central Park contains the highest concentration of Victorian houses in the country.

The city's standout museum is the Muhammad Ali Center, which goes far deeper into the message and beliefs of the man than just presenting his boxing career. Nearby, the Louisville Slugger Museum is actually an active baseball-bat factory, which offers entertaining tours and a miniature bat at the end. Further afield, adjacent to Churchill Downs racecourse, the Kentucky Derby Museum tells you everything you need to know about the legendary race. Nor do you have to venture far beyond the urban area to find yourself in the heart of Bourbon Country, home to some of the nation's best-loved distilleries.

Louisville Slugger Museum & Factory

The Kentucky Derby

Muhammad Ali Center

Maker's Mark Distillery

Broadway in Mammoth Cave

Entrance to Mammoth Cave National Park

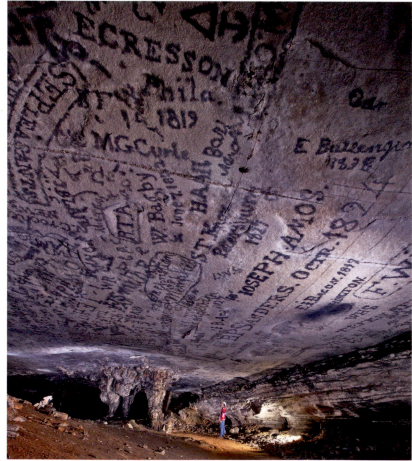

Historic signatures adorn the ceiling in Gothic Avenue

Green River

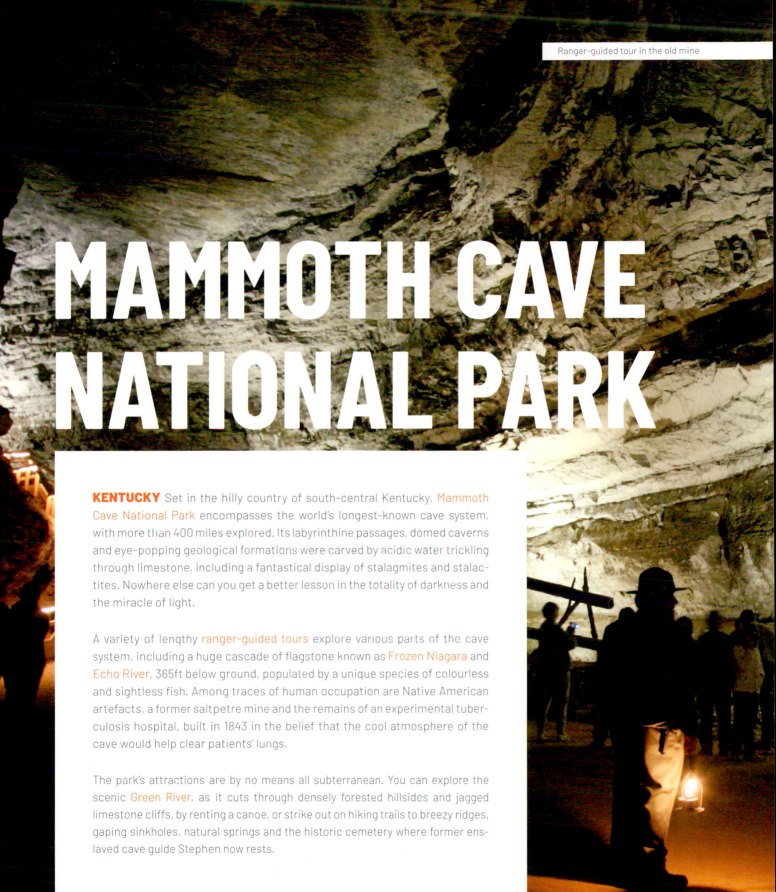

MAMMOTH CAVE NATIONAL PARK

KENTUCKY Set in the hilly country of south-central Kentucky, Mammoth Cave National Park encompasses the world's longest-known cave system, with more than 400 miles explored. Its labyrinthine passages, domed caverns and eye-popping geological formations were carved by acidic water trickling through limestone, including a fantastical display of stalagmites and stalactites. Nowhere else can you get a better lesson in the totality of darkness and the miracle of light.

A variety of lengthy ranger-guided tours explore various parts of the cave system, including a huge cascade of flagstone known as Frozen Niagara and Echo River, 365ft below ground, populated by a unique species of colourless and sightless fish. Among traces of human occupation are Native American artefacts, a former saltpetre mine and the remains of an experimental tuberculosis hospital, built in 1843 in the belief that the cool atmosphere of the cave would help clear patients' lungs.

The park's attractions are by no means all subterranean. You can explore the scenic Green River, as it cuts through densely forested hillsides and jagged limestone cliffs, by renting a canoe, or strike out on hiking trails to breezy ridges, gaping sinkholes, natural springs and the historic cemetery where former enslaved cave guide Stephen now rests.

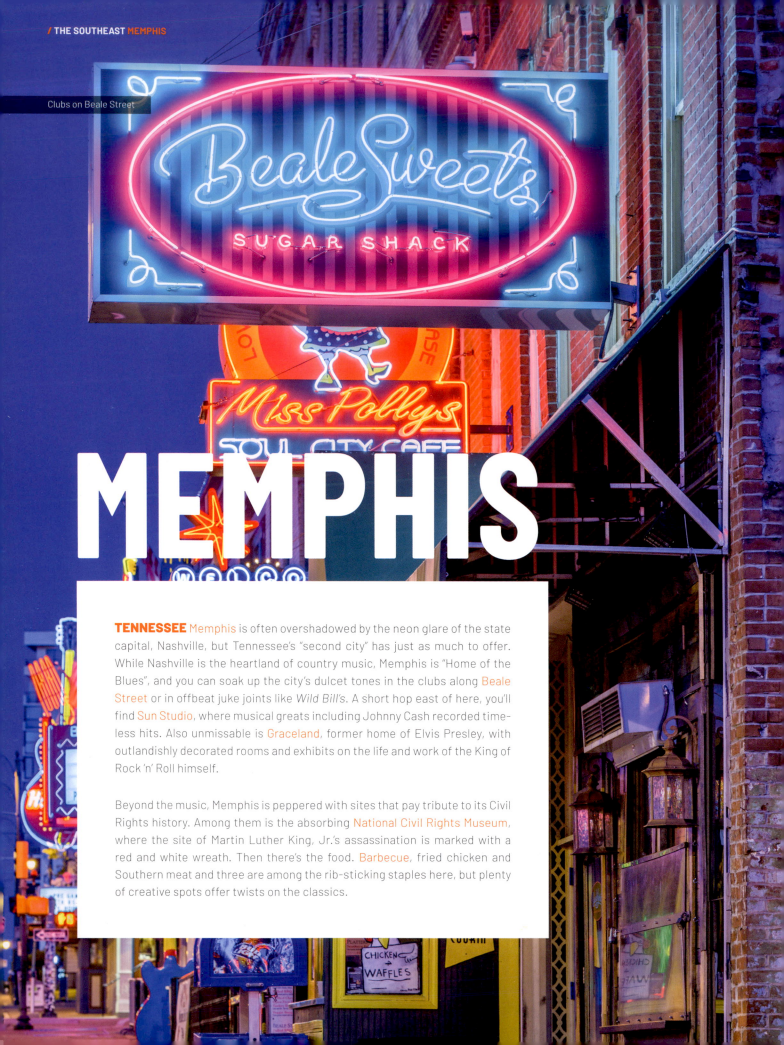

Clubs on Beale Street

MEMPHIS

TENNESSEE Memphis is often overshadowed by the neon glare of the state capital, Nashville, but Tennessee's "second city" has just as much to offer. While Nashville is the heartland of country music, Memphis is "Home of the Blues", and you can soak up the city's dulcet tones in the clubs along Beale Street or in offbeat juke joints like *Wild Bill's*. A short hop east of here, you'll find Sun Studio, where musical greats including Johnny Cash recorded timeless hits. Also unmissable is Graceland, former home of Elvis Presley, with outlandishly decorated rooms and exhibits on the life and work of the King of Rock 'n' Roll himself.

Beyond the music, Memphis is peppered with sites that pay tribute to its Civil Rights history. Among them is the absorbing National Civil Rights Museum, where the site of Martin Luther King, Jr.'s assassination is marked with a red and white wreath. Then there's the food. Barbecue, fried chicken and Southern meat and three are among the rib-sticking staples here, but plenty of creative spots offer twists on the classics.

Sun Studio

Eating at Gus's World Famous Fried Chicken

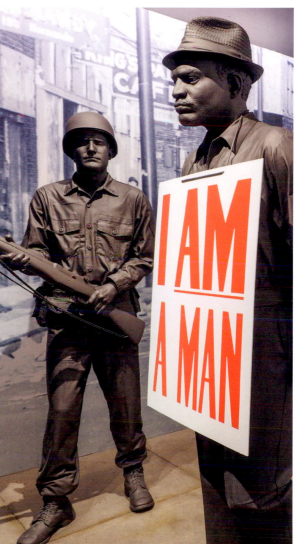

The Pool Room in Elvis Presley's Graceland

National Civil Rights Museum

Mural in Wynwood Art District

Art Deco architecture on Ocean Drive

Rooftop bar overlooking Brickell Avenue

Little Havana

MIAMI

FLORIDA If it's swaying palms, bronzed roller-skaters and show-stealing life-guard huts you're after, Miami doesn't disappoint – but there are plenty of other highlights in the city, too. Stylish pastel-hued hotels pepper the South Beach area, where Art Deco walking tours bring their glamorous and scandalous histories to life.

A short way across the river is Little Havana, a quiet neighbourhood which has been home to a large and colourful Cuban community since the 1950s. Along its main drag, SW 8th Street (or Calle Ocho), hip-swaying salsa bars, authentic restaurants and quiet Cuban cafés jostle for space. Neighbouring Wynwood Art District is vibrant and charged: almost every visible edifice is decorated with murals, stickers and spray-painted portraits, from the likes of Melania Trump to Amy Winehouse. While you can take guided tours around the original Wynwood Walls, as they're so dwarfed by the rest of the neighbourhood's artworks, you can simply wander through the district and take it all in by yourself. To round it off, it wouldn't be a quintessential Miami experience without sipping a *Cuba Libre* at a rooftop bar or kayaking past celebrity houses along Star Island – you might even be lucky enough to spot a dolphin or two.

Classic car in the South Beach area

On the beach

State reptile loggerhead turtle nests are protected by law

The Ferris wheel at night at Broadway at the Beach

Family Kingdom Amusement Park

MYRTLE BEACH

SOUTH CAROLINA Founded by a mix of European settlers in the late-eighteenth century, Myrtle Beach is the hub of the 60-mile Grand Strand coast that connects Georgetown to the northern tip of South Carolina. In its early days, the settlement's remoteness made it impossible for Myrtle Beach to benefit from the usual economies of the era, trading in indigo and tobacco. Instead, the focus was tourism, fuelled by the arrival of the railway in 1900.

Today, that economy thrives on golf courses, state-park campgrounds, fishing trips, watersports and even a Dolly Parton backed, Vegas-esque, all-singing-and-swashbuckling pirate dinner and show. Look out for the Myrtle Beach Pavilion Amusement Park – home to a vintage Herschel-Spillman merry-go-round. Dating back to 1908, it's a rare example of a hand-carved carousel.

What makes this stretch of the South Carolina coast most special, however, is its role as a safe haven for endangered sea turtles to lay their eggs – which they do here en masse each spring. Turtle-related tourism has been channelled to support wildlife conservation, and though it might not be everyone's tasteful cup of tea, the dollars it attracts are crucial to the survival of these beautiful creatures.

NEW ORLEANS

LOUISIANA Infused with a dizzying jumble of cultures and influences, New Orleans is a bewitching place. Here, people dance at funerals and hold parties during hurricanes, world-class musicians make ends meet busking on street corners and hole-in-the-wall dives dish up gourmet Creole cuisine.

A solo saxophone, a blasting brass number, the ring-a-ting-ting of a snare drum – this is the rhythm of New Orleans. It's jazz the city is most famous for, but you'll find plenty of rousing R&B, gospel, blues, funk and soul as well. There's a wistfulness here too, along with its famed *joie de vivre* – in the peeling facades of the old French Quarter, its filigree cast-iron balconies tangled with ferns and fragrant jasmine, and in the cemeteries lined with crumbling above-ground marble tombs. And then there's Mardi Gras. Striking parades and electric energy tear up the city streets, where masked revellers party till dawn. Recently a grand 300-years-old, New Orleans's addictive musicality keeps ringing out, and it's as loud as ever.

SIDEWALK
CLOSED
HERE

The French Quarter

OUTER BANKS

NORTH CAROLINA A string of skinny barrier islands, the remnants of ancient sand dunes, the Outer Banks stretch about 180 miles from the Virginia border to Cape Lookout. Easily navigable by bridges, seafood shack-lined avenues and lonely highways, it's a great region to meander, with wonderful wild beaches, otherworldly salt marshes and attractive small towns such as Kitty Hawk, Kill Devil Hills and Nags Head. This trio are still mostly beautifully unspoiled, yet in high summer season quite touristy. In Nags Head, Jockey's Ridge State Park boasts the largest sand dunes on the East Coast, which are eerily lovely at sunset. Walking downhill is like clomping through a warm snowbank – a surreal and highly enjoyable experience. Roanoke Island, meanwhile, site of the first English settlement in the USA (which vanished inexplicably in 1590) has obvious historical interest; its village, Manteo, is one of the nicest on the Outer Banks.

Nags Head beach from the pier

Dune at Jockey's Ridge State Park

Bodie Island Lighthouse and boardwalk

Great blue heron at sunrise

La Coca Falls in El Yunque National Forest

Calle San Sebastián in Old San Juan

Hammocks sway gently on a sunny beach

PUERTO RICO

UNINCORPORATED TERRITORIES Vibrant Puerto Rico has been an unincorporated territory of the United States since 1898. Today, this captivating Caribbean island dances to a diverse tune, with the stunning sixteenth-century Spanish architecture of cosmopolitan capital San Juan at its historic heart. Alongside legacies of its colonial era, Puerto Rico has plenty of important pre-Columbian attractions, among them Caguana Indigenous Ceremonial Park in the north, and Tibes Indigenous Ceremonial Center near Ponce in the south. Offering insights into the island's indigenous Taíno, these are considered to be among the most significant archeological sites in the Caribbean.

The only tropical rainforest in the US National Forest network, El Yunque is a must-visit for nature-lovers, and key to the survival of the endemic Puerto Rican parrot. Wiped-out in the wild by Hurricanes Irma and Maria in 2017, captive-bred Puerto Rican parrots have now been successfully introduced to this biologically diverse forest.

Surfers should head to the wild-waved, west coast region of Rincón, while calm, crystalline waters welcome visitors to Playa Flamenco on the island of Culebra, some seventeen miles off the mainland. Named after a nearby lagoon that attracts flamingos in winter, Playa Flamenco is frequently feted as one of the world's best beaches.

Savannah Riverfront

SAVANNAH

GEORGIA American towns don't come much more beautiful than Savannah, seventeen miles up the Savannah River from the ocean. The ravishing historic district, arranged around Spanish-moss-swathed garden squares, formed the core of the original city and boasts examples of just about every architectural style of the eighteenth and nineteenth centuries, while the cobbled waterfront on the Savannah River is edged by towering old cotton warehouses. Savannah's historic district is flanked by the river to the north, Martin Luther King, Jr. Boulevard to the west, Gaston Street to the south and Broad Street to the east. The main draw here is in wandering the side streets and admiring the shuttered Federal, Regency and antebellum houses, embellished with intricate iron balconies. More than twenty residential squares, shaded by canopies of ancient live oaks and ablaze with dogwood trees, azaleas and creamy magnolias, offer peaceful respite from the blistering summer heat, while subtropical greenery creeps its way through the ornate railings, cracks open the streets, casts cool shadows and fills the air with its warm, sensual fragrance.

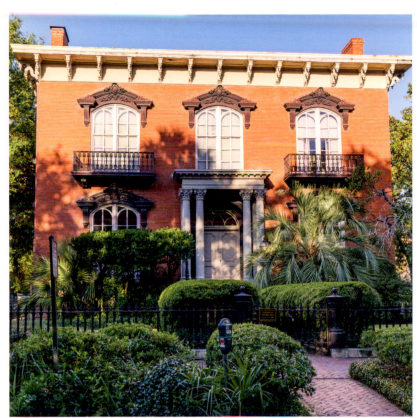

Mercer-Williams House Museum

Bonaventure Cemetery

Monterey Square

Ballastone Inn

St George Street

A re-enactor in St Augustine

Flagler College

Lion statue on Bridge of Lions

ST AUGUSTINE

FLORIDA America's oldest and arguably most beautiful city is peppered with Spanish fortifications and threaded by quaint cobbled streets – as well as hosting a pirate-treasure museum – all baked under the soft Florida sun. Established forty years before the first English settlement in Jamestown and 55-years before the Pilgrims arrived on the *Mayflower* in Massachusetts, St Augustine is a rare nod to America's little-known Spanish roots. Founded in 1565 by Spanish general Pedro Menéndez de Avilés, the heavily fortified Castillo de San Marcos is the only remnant of the original city, thanks largely to devastating attacks by the British navy – led by Sir Francis Drake – and pirates, including the notorious Robert Searle.

Aside from the pomp of the Castillo, with its tour guides dressed in military uniforms and firing cannons, this is a quiet little city sprinkled with basilicas, plazas, coffee shops, hole in the walls and tapas restaurants, most of which you'll find along St George Street – the old entrance to the city, marked by the crumbling coquina pillars from the original city gate. There's also the famed Fountain of Youth nearby. This mineral spring was discovered by explorer Ponce de León, who lauded the sulphuric waters for their alleged healing and age-reversing powers.

Castillo de San Marcos

The Eternal Flame, Martin Luther King, Jr. National Historic Site

Grave of Martin Luther King, Jr. and his spouse Coretta Scott King

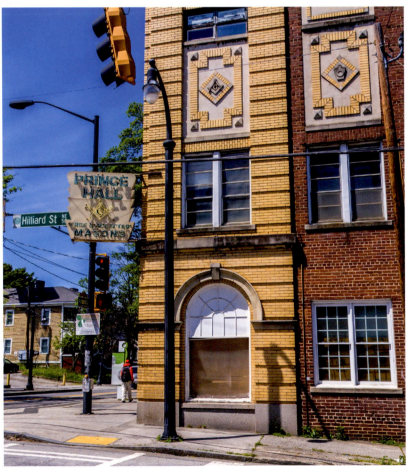

Prince Hall Masonic Temple

Historic Ebenezer Baptist Church

The childhood home of Martin Luther King, Jr.

SWEET AUBURN

GEORGIA Mark Twain put it best, as early as 1882: "In the South, the [Civil] war is what AD is elsewhere; they date everything from it". Several generations later, the legacies of slavery and "The War Between the States" remain evident throughout the southern heartlands, and it's impossible to travel through the region without experiencing constant reminders of the two epic historical clashes that have shaped its destiny: the Civil War, and the civil rights movement of the 1950s and 1960s. In Atlanta, Georgia, you'll find one of the South's most powerful sights – and one inextricably linked to its violent past.

Auburn Avenue stands as a monument to Atlanta's black history. During its heyday in the 1920s, "Sweet Auburn" was a prosperous, progressive area of black-owned businesses and jazz clubs, but it went into decline with the Depression from which it never truly recovered. Several blocks have been designated as the Martin Luther King, Jr. National Historic Site, in honour of Auburn's most cherished native son. This short stretch of road is the most visited attraction in Georgia and it's a moving experience to watch the crowds of school kids waiting in turn to take photographs.

WALT DISNEY WORLD

FLORIDA The biggest and cleverest theme-park complex ever created, Walt Disney World turned a wedge of Florida farmland into one of the planet's most lucrative holiday destinations almost overnight.

'It's a Small World (After All)' plays on repeat as log flumes bob through the make-believe world of Splash Mountain, one of the Magic Kingdom's most iconic rides. Beloved princess, gallant knights and a whole host of creatures great and small roam the quaint streets here, where Micky mingles with the crowds and Cinderella stops for selfies. But the Magic Kingdom is just one of four theme parks making up this fantasy land, where childhoods can be relived and brought to life.

Animal Kingdom, the most relaxed of the four, offers excursions into the wild, from safaris in the African plains to riding the rapids of India's Kali River. Known for its giant, golfball-like geosphere, Epcot is Disney's celebration of science, technology and world cultures. Occupying the largest area of the park is World Showcase, which transports visitors across the globe with elaborate re-creations of different countries, from Japan (think: geishas) to Norway (Vikings). Explore movie sets and mix with the stars at Disney's Hollywood Studios, and end the evening with the spectacular firework display that fizzes over Epcot.

Mickey Mouse and Minnie Mouse wave hello

WINDSOR PLANTATION RUINS

MISSISSIPPI Along a quiet, dusty road from Port Gibson, a cluster of 23 surviving columns stand tall, topped by Corinthian capitals. Although the stucco is crumbling away, it's clear that at one time these belonged to an exquisite building. In fact, Windsor Plantation, built in 1861, was once considered the largest and finest mansion in all of Mississippi. What today appears incongruous in a wild land, straddled by creeks and bayous that empty into the mighty Mississippi nearby, stood "visible for miles in every direction" – according to Mark Twain.

Something about the demise of the vast mansion, the heart of an old cotton plantation, seems fitting, evocative of an era when human beings were bought and sold, then forced to work the land against their will. Several Civil War battles that eventually put paid to slavery in America were fought in this area; Union soldiers only spared Windsor because of its grandeur. Instead, a carelessly discarded cigar butt set the building alight in 1890, bringing it to the ruin you see today. The sweeping cotton fields are largely overgrown now, replaced by clumps of ash and willow, but stand amid these ruins and you can almost hear the defiant songs of the Underground Railroad drift over the land.

The columns of Windsor Ruins

THE
SOUTHWEST

AUSTIN

TEXAS The Texas state capital of Austin – now one of the nation's fastest-growing and most attractive cities – has cemented its popularity by making numerous Top 10 lists in the US in recent years: coolest, best college town, best for doing business, fastest-growing tech centre, best to retire, best for live music and culture, best barbecue, best to visit... the list goes on. Suffice to say: Austin is where it's at.

Booming downtown redevelopment, a burgeoning jobs market and growth on every front are the results of Austin's double act as both state and true cultural capital. These strange bedfellows have helped secure Austin's reputation as one of America's top "creative cities", a term coined by sociologist Richard Florida to describe the unique mix of jobs, culture, services, affordable housing, liveability and general exuberance that makes a city so interesting to creatives. This is the home of Whole Foods, hipsters, South by Southwest, movie stars, localism and the University of Texas (UT) – a bastion of liberal politics and environmentalism surrounded by a conservative state whose demographics are rapidly changing in Austin's favour. Just about everything is on the table.

Cosmic Coffee + Beer Garden sign

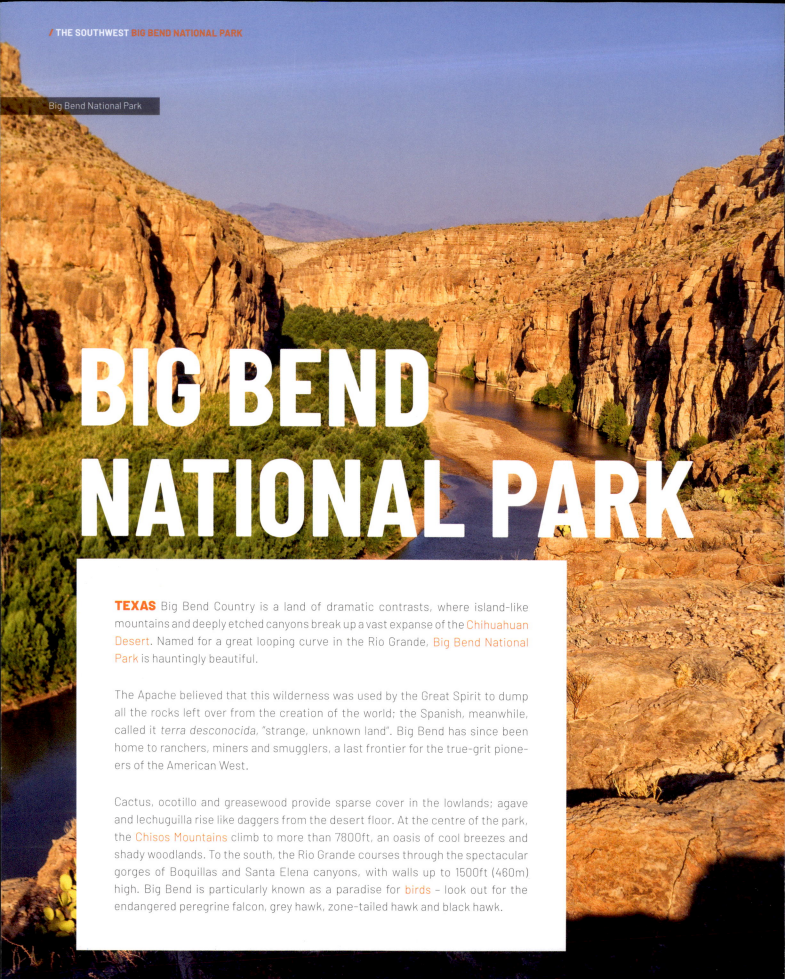

Big Bend National Park

BIG BEND NATIONAL PARK

TEXAS Big Bend Country is a land of dramatic contrasts, where island-like mountains and deeply etched canyons break up a vast expanse of the Chihuahuan Desert. Named for a great looping curve in the Rio Grande, Big Bend National Park is hauntingly beautiful.

The Apache believed that this wilderness was used by the Great Spirit to dump all the rocks left over from the creation of the world; the Spanish, meanwhile, called it *terra desconocida*, "strange, unknown land". Big Bend has since been home to ranchers, miners and smugglers, a last frontier for the true-grit pioneers of the American West.

Cactus, ocotillo and greasewood provide sparse cover in the lowlands; agave and lechuguilla rise like daggers from the desert floor. At the centre of the park, the Chisos Mountains climb to more than 7800ft, an oasis of cool breezes and shady woodlands. To the south, the Rio Grande courses through the spectacular gorges of Boquillas and Santa Elena canyons, with walls up to 1500ft (460m) high. Big Bend is particularly known as a paradise for birds – look out for the endangered peregrine falcon, grey hawk, zone-tailed hawk and black hawk.

Unique rock stack formations

Pink cacti

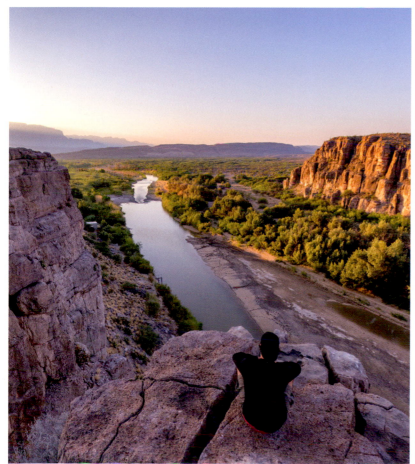

The Rio Grande river

Giant dagger yucca

Overlooking Calf Creek Falls

A small waterfall and pool above Upper Calf Creek Falls

Lower Calf Creek Falls trail

Upper Calf Creek Falls

CALF CREEK FALLS

UTAH Indisputably the most scenic of southern Utah's dozen "Scenic Byways", Hwy-12 connects Bryce Canyon and Capitol Reef national parks. Halfway along its panoply of red-rock canyons, crystal-clear rivers and shimmering oases, two superb waterfalls offer the perfect opportunity to explore on foot.

Reaching the stupendous 125ft Lower Calf Creek Falls entails a magnificent six-mile round-trip hike. Heading upstream between high red canyon walls, the trail follows a perennial creek, interrupted by beaver ponds. The falls

finally appear, spilling over the pouting lip of a crevice in a vast sandstone amphitheatre, and spreading across a mossy slope of golden stone, iridescent with rainbows. The (freezing) pool below is fringed by a shaded beach; rest before hiking back out.

The hike to the smaller Upper Calf Creek Falls, from a separate trailhead six miles north, makes a quicker, if more challenging, alternative. For the first mile, as you cross exposed slickrock, the slope may seem intimidating, but with good boots it's not hard, and the views are amazing. When you sense the location of the stream, bear right. Eventually, the trail forks: one strand goes to the top of the 50ft falls, the other to the bottom, where another lovely pool awaits.

Lower Calf Creek Falls

El Capitan in the Guadalupe Mountains National Park

The Dollhouse in Carlsbad Caverns

Stalagmites in the caverns

CARLSBAD CAVERNS AND GUADALUPE MOUNTAINS NATIONAL PARKS

NEW MEXICO/TEXAS Southeastern New Mexico and West Texas sit in the Permian Basin, famed for its huge oil reserves and historic ranches along the US–Mexico border.

If the region's torrid Chihuahuan Desert somehow feels oceanic, that's because, 265 million years ago, this landscape was covered by the warm, shallow Permian sea. The skeletons of dead marine creatures gradually accreted into a coral reef, which was later buried by oil-rich shales, uplifted and eroded into the Guadalupes, the highest mountains and largest wilderness in Texas. Meanwhile, in New Mexico, acidic groundwater carved an extensive cave system into the Permian Reef at Carlsbad Caverns, whose dripping surfaces became decorated by precipitated limestone stalagmites, stalactites, helectites and other fantastical features.

The shady campground in the Guadalupes makes a good base. In fall, hikers enjoy blazing colours in historic McKittrick Canyon and sweeping views from 8749ft Guadalupe Peak, while in summer, the cool temperatures in Carlsbad Caverns offer respite. Access the Big Room by elevator to view the main cavern, or walk the steep Natural Entrance trail, where a colony of bats resides. Ranger-led tours of "wild caves", as their cowboy discoverer Jim White and National Geographic explorers saw them, offer real caving experiences for the adventurous.

GRAND CANYON

ARIZONA Although almost five million people visit Grand Canyon National Park every year, the canyon itself remains beyond the grasp of human imagination. No photograph, no statistics, can prepare you for such immensity. Billions of years of the earth's geologic history is frozen in bright bands of pink, beige, orange, rust and gold on the canyon walls. Peer into the abyss to glimpse a sliver of the Colorado River, nearly 2km below, which carved out the canyon some six billion years ago. By contrast, the national park – a UNESCO World Heritage Site – has only just past the century mark.

Spend at least a full day here, watching the colours change in the shifting light. The vast majority of visitors come to the South Rim and linger at the viewpoints, spotting rare California condors soaring on the breeze, though the North Rim can be a lot more evocative by virtue of its isolation. Wherever you go, you are gazing at one of the Seven Wonders of the Natural World. Breathe it in.

A Grand Canyon sunrise

The Great Ghost cluster

Admiring the findings at the Great Gallery

Detail of the pictographs

Horseshoe Canyon

Hiking through Horseshoe Canyon

GREAT GALLERY

UTAH Gorgeous Horseshoe Canyon, a remote chunk of Canyonlands National Park, is home to the most extraordinary rock art in North America. No one now knows the meaning of the mysterious, haunting figures that line its walls. Although to the modern eye they suggest an astonishing sophistication, they're among the oldest such images to survive, painted between 1600 and 6000 years ago.

Having first driven 42 dirt-road miles southeast of Green River, Utah, you have to hike seven exposed but sublimely beautiful miles (round-trip) to see the Great Gallery itself. Crossing patches of deep sand alternating with slickrock, the trail descends to the floor of Horseshoe Canyon. After an hour of twisting and turning beneath towering cliffs, you round the final bend to meet a long row of dark, hollow-eyed, otherworldly entities, stark against the pale rock of a sandstone overhang. It's a breathtaking moment. Roughly life-sized but weirdly elongated, these anthropomorphic figures often lack both arms and legs. Some have large round eyes, others simply empty sockets, while many seem draped in stylized robes; the cumulative effect is to suggest ghosts or spirits from another, very different time.

The Golden Nugget Las Vegas and Plaza Hotel & Casino

Inside the Luxor Hotel & Casino

View over the Strip

Vegas Vickie sign at the Circa Resort & Casino

LAS VEGAS

NEVADA A dazzling oasis where about forty million people a year escape the everyday, Las Vegas will blow your mind as well as your wallet. From its ever-changing architecture to cascading chocolate fountains, adrenaline-pumping zip lines and jaw-dropping stage shows, everything is built to thrill; as soon as the novelty wears off, it's blown up and replaced with something bigger and better. The city of excess is home to many of the largest hotels in the world – and that's pretty much all – but it's these extraordinary creations everyone comes to see.

Each hotel is a neighbourhood in its own right, measuring as much as a mile end to end; crammed full of state-of-the-art clubs, restaurants, spas and pools; and centring on what makes the whole thing possible – an action-packed casino where tourists and tycoons alike are gripped by the roll of the dice and the turn of a card.

Binoculars mounted to poles at Marfa Lights viewing area

Marfa gasoline art

A modernist adobe residence in Marfa

Neon art

MARFA

TEXAS Marfa, a small but thriving community 21 miles south of Fort Davis in Texas, is the kind of place that is at once hard to imagine existing where it is, but also existing anywhere else. It is very much a desert oasis, with a respected art scene pulling artists and the curious from afar in increasing numbers.

It's also a decidedly offbeat town, where chic designer shops and prefab galleries are offset by historic buildings that attest to its former role as a ranching centre. It all makes for a fascinating mix. Much more ethereal, the Marfa Lights, a few miles east of town, consistently draw crowds, even if the lights don't always cooperate. Since the 1880s, these mysterious bouncing lights have been seen in the town's flat fields – they've long attracted conspiracy theorists and alien-hunters, though their cause may be more prosaic.

Roadside sign for Marfa Hill House

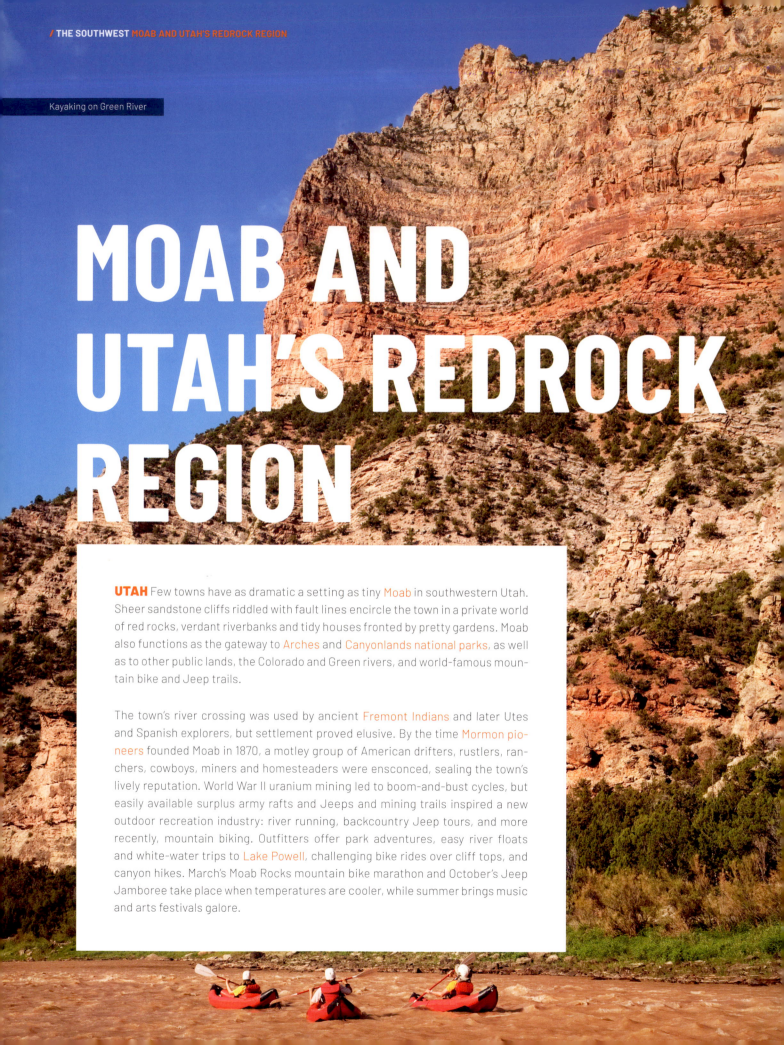

Kayaking on Green River

MOAB AND UTAH'S REDROCK REGION

UTAH Few towns have as dramatic a setting as tiny Moab in southwestern Utah. Sheer sandstone cliffs riddled with fault lines encircle the town in a private world of red rocks, verdant riverbanks and tidy houses fronted by pretty gardens. Moab also functions as the gateway to Arches and Canyonlands national parks, as well as to other public lands, the Colorado and Green rivers, and world-famous mountain bike and Jeep trails.

The town's river crossing was used by ancient Fremont Indians and later Utes and Spanish explorers, but settlement proved elusive. By the time Mormon pioneers founded Moab in 1870, a motley group of American drifters, rustlers, ranchers, cowboys, miners and homesteaders were ensconced, sealing the town's lively reputation. World War II uranium mining led to boom-and-bust cycles, but easily available surplus army rafts and Jeeps and mining trails inspired a new outdoor recreation industry: river running, backcountry Jeep tours, and more recently, mountain biking. Outfitters offer park adventures, easy river floats and white-water trips to Lake Powell, challenging bike rides over cliff tops, and canyon hikes. March's Moab Rocks mountain bike marathon and October's Jeep Jamboree take place when temperatures are cooler, while summer brings music and arts festivals galore.

Moab jeep tour

Bowtie Arch, a 'pothole arch' near Moab

Mountain biking Slickrock Trail in Moab

MONUMENT VALLEY

UTAH From Stagecoach to Buster Scruggs, Monument Valley has been immortalized on the silver screen from the earliest days of Hollywood cinema. This tract of rugged wilderness epitomizes both the Wild West's endless allure and its mortal fragility, but these huge sandstone buttes, rising up from the arid red desert, are actually the product of millions of years of climatic attrition.

Long before any European set eyes on – or gave the current name to – Monument Valley, the natural wonders were already considered sacred by the Navajo Nation, and are now encompassed by their wider ancestral lands.

This whole region is best experienced by driving along the open road. Better yet, access restricted areas by joining a guided horseback tour, travelling through the canyons the traditional way. Nearby, amid other geological marvels – natural stone arches and the like – is the occasional prehistoric cave dwelling, proof that this seemingly inhospitable region has enchanted humans for millennia.

View over Hunts Mesa, Monument Valley

Spring wildflowers in the Wasatch Mountains

NORTHERN UTAH

UTAH Rugged rocks and rust-red plains probably come to mind when you think of Utah – and that's true of the state's south, home to big hitters such as Bryce Canyon and Zion National Park. But strike north, away from the hordes down south, and you'll find a land of fir tree-covered mountains and green valleys, which are both wildly underrated and blissfully crowd free.

Here you can drive an ATV through the peaks of Wasatch Mountain State Park, pausing to look down on the lush plains of Heber Valley, or stroll through the chocolate-box ski town of Park City. Head farther north still, to the Idaho border, and you'll reach Bear Lake, dubbed the "Caribbean of the Rockies" for its popping expanse of blue.

A stone's throw from Salt Lake City, the state's capital, you'll also find Antelope Island, an epic wilderness jutting into Utah's Great Salt Lake. This is the place to come for back-country hiking and to spot big-horn sheep and free-roaming bison. It's also an International Dark Sky Park: stars freckle inky skies after dark, and monthly events draw budding astronomers.

Park City

Mountain road with autumnal colours, Wasatch Mountains

Wild American bison on the grasslands of Antelope Island

Sunset landscape, Great Salt Lake

Wooden ladder at the site

Petroglyphs

Pottery fragments at the site

View over all the dwellings

Tours are like Snakes and Ladders - you climb up the levels via ladders

PUYÉ CLIFF DWELLINGS

NEW MEXICO A thousand years ago, the so-called Ancestral Puebloans lived throughout the Four Corners region, where Arizona and Utah meet Colorado and New Mexico. Their long-abandoned "cliff dwellings" now form the starring attractions in national parks and monuments such as Mesa Verde (see page 181), Bandelier and Canyon de Chelley. What's extraordinary about New Mexico's little-known Puyé Cliff Dwellings, however, is that their original native American inhabitants still live very close at hand, in adjoining Santa Clara Pueblo, and now lead visitors on fascinating guided tours. It's rare indeed to hear such a site interpreted by members of the self-same group that used to occupy it.

Consisting of two tiers of "apartments" hollowed into a south-facing canyon wall – soft enough to be shaped with wooden tools – the dwellings were occupied between 1250 and 1550. Intriguingly, petroglyphs above the entrances appear to mark specific homes, though in fact those that survived were originally interior rooms in larger complexes, fronted by adobe-walled structures. Tours resemble a real-life game of Snakes and Ladders; you climb from level to level via steep wooden ladders – and yes, you might encounter snakes sunning themselves on the pathways.

Gila woodpeckers

Saguaro cactus flowers in bloom

Sunset over Saguaro National Park

Tall saguaros

SAGUARO NATIONAL PARK

ARIZONA Encompassing stretches of the arid Sonoran Desert in southeastern Arizona, Saguaro National Park offers visitors a rare and enthralling opportunity to stroll through desert "forests" of colossal, multilimbed saguaro cactuses. These can grow up to 50ft tall, reaching full height after around 150 years. Between late April and June, saguaros sprout up to one hundred white flowers, each of which blossoms for a single night. Woodpeckers and owls burrow holes into the trunk for their nests, while the Tohono O'odham people mashed the saguaro's succulent crimson fruit to make jam, syrup and even wine, and used its long, wood-like ribs to construct dwellings and fences.

The Tucson Mountain District of the park is traversed by the Bajada Loop Drive, which wriggles through a wonderland of twisted saguaro. The easiest walk, the Desert Discovery Nature Trail, follows a small gully before climbing onto a low brow for sweeping westward views. Further along the road lies Signal Hill, known for its magnificent sunset panoramas. The eastern section of the park, the Rincon Mountain District, is accessed by Cactus Forest Loop Drive. From the road, the Freeman Homestead Trail drops down to the barely visible vestiges of a pioneer home, then follows the course of a gentle wash back up again, threading between abundant groups of towering saguaro.

Adobe Pueblo Revival architecture of Inn and Spa at Loretto

SANTA FE

NEW MEXICO They call Santa Fe the "City Different" – a unique salsa of art, history and culture served up at the foot of New Mexico's sparkling Sangre de Cristo mountains. It's this combination, including the spectacular setting, that lures artists, writers, dancers, musicians, foodies, film makers, New Age seekers and history buffs alike. Built atop an ancient pueblo in 1610, Santa Fe has seen the flags of three countries – Spain, Mexico and the United States – fly over the adobe Governor's Palace on the Plaza, and the city remains a multicultural oasis today. World-famous Indian, Spanish, Folk Art and far-mer's markets, a renowned opera company and trippy art experience Meow Wolf are just the start. You'll find a hundred art galleries on quaint Canyon Road and a hundred more beyond it, scores of traditional and innovative restaurants, a dozen cultural museums, and the second-highest per-capita artist population in the world in America's first UNESCO creative community.

Further afield you can visit historic cave dwellings, hike and ski in the moun-tains, soak in hot springs, watch weavers in Hispanic villages and attend ceremonial dances at an Indian pueblo. Just don't forget to slow down and lose yourself in the timeless *duende* (magic) of Santa Fe – and, of course, ask for green chilli on everything.

Canyon Road art gallery

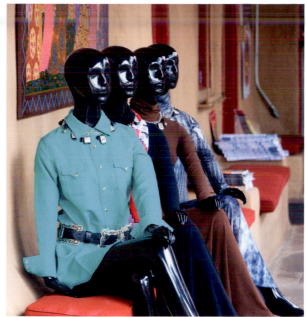

Santa Fe fashion

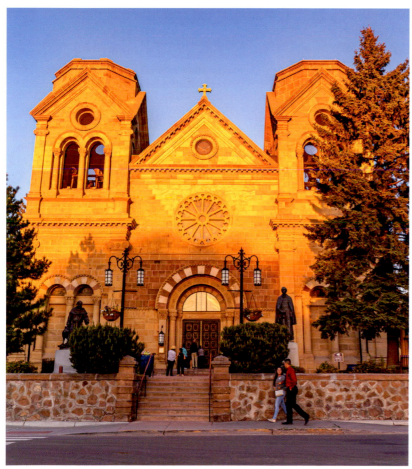

Cathedral Basilica of Saint Francis of Assisi

Painted columns in the downtown plaza

TOMBSTONE AND BISBEE

ARIZONA Set just twenty miles apart in Arizona's flyblown southeastern desert, these two neighbouring towns offer amazingly contrasting flavours of the Wild West. Each prospered from mining, but has experienced a very different afterlife. Tombstone, where a huge 1878 silver strike panned out within ten years, and Wyatt Earp and Doc Halliday gunned down the Clanton gang at the OK Corral, is now in essence an entertaining but still-authentic theme park. Ornery gunslingers stage regular shoot-outs on its dusty streets and wooden sidewalks, while the Clantons lie buried in the evocative Boothill Cemetery.

The fortunes of nearby Bisbee, by contrast, were built on a century of extracting mundane, dependable copper, discovered in the surrounding mountains in 1877. Briefly the largest city between New Orleans and San Francisco, it remains among Arizona's most atmospheric Victorian towns. When the miners moved away, after its vast open-pit mine finally closed in 1975, artists and retirees moved in, turning Bisbee into a thriving, friendly little community that's filled with B&Bs and restaurants. The best lodging of all is at the *Shady Dell*, where guests sleep in beautifully restored, irresistibly kitsch 1950s trailers.

Tombstone gunfight

Stagecoach tour of Tombstone

View over Bisbee

Boothill Cemetery in Tombstone

Road through Valley of Fire State Park

Rabbit shaped rock formation

Bighorn sheep in the park

Red and beige bands of rock

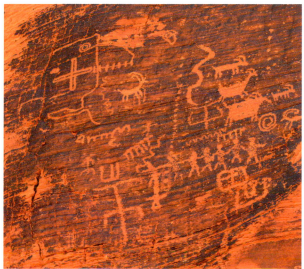

Petroglyphs

VALLEY OF FIRE STATE PARK

NEVADA Some say that the sun reflecting off the curious rock formations in the Valley of Fire looks like a sea of flame; others that the rocks resemble elephants, spears, beehives and even a huddle of shy sisters. One thing is certain: look closely, and the eroded sandstone outcrops tell many stories. Petroglyphs etched onto canyon walls by the Basketmaker people centuries ago act as an ancient artistic guide to the land, showing where to drink, eat and sleep.

Elsewhere, striated red and beige bands of hardened sediment are testament to the slow twists and compressions of ceaseless geology. Petrified logs poking through the ground hint at millennia spent trapped under the silt of seasonal rivers. Sandy trails wind through russet slot canyons, whose walls are pockmarked by round weathered crevices like compound eyes.

Along one of the park's many hiking routes you might come across the desert tortoise, bighorn sheep, coyotes or the cartoonish roadrunner in among the creosote and cacti – each one proving that, against the odds, life thrives in the Valley of Fire.

WHITE SANDS NATIONAL PARK

NEW MEXICO Otherworldly enough to double as David Bowie's home planet in *The Man Who Fell To Earth*, the dazzling dunes of White Sands fill 275 square miles of southern New Mexico. Deposited on an ancient seabed 250 million years ago, they're not in fact sand but fine gypsum. Anywhere else, they would have dissolved and been carried off by rivers; here, there are none.

Driving in, you enter a bizarre world of knife-edge ridges and graceful slopes. Roadside pull-outs, equipped with fabulous 1950s-style curving picnic shelters, enable you to leave your vehicle and wade through pristine sand to the top of the ridges, before slipping and sliding back down. Hiking into the wilderness is all but irresistible, but keep your bearings, and carry at least a gallon of water per person; running out of water can be fatal.

To add to the sense of mystery, this remote region holds an active missile range – the first-ever atomic bomb was detonated here in July 1945 – and road access closes for short periods during tests.

Flowers in White Sands National Park

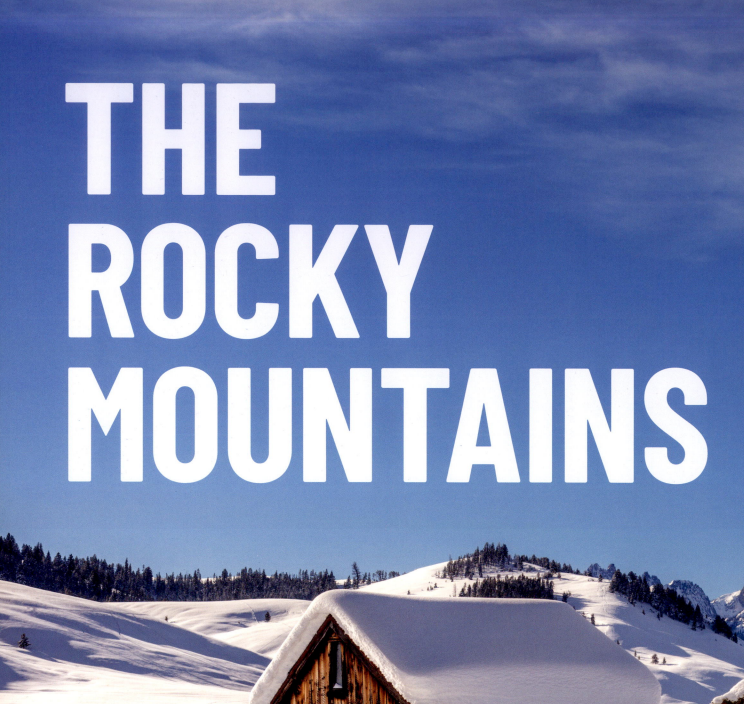

THE ROCKY MOUNTAINS

Denver's skyline with the Rockies behind

DENVER

COLORADO Its substantial ensemble of glittering skyscrapers marking the final transition between the Great Plains and the American West, Denver stands at the threshold of the Rocky Mountains. Though clearly visible from downtown, the majestic peaks of the Front Range start to rise roughly fifteen miles west, and the "Mile High City" (at an elevation of 5280ft) is itself uniformly flat.

The nightlife in Denver is second to none, with dozens of great bars and restaurants oozing laidback, Colorado cool. Its lively arts scene, from the architecturally stunning Denver Art Museum to the vivid street murals of the RiNo District, will take a leap into the cutting edge with the opening of Meow Wolf, a mind-blowing immersive art installation. To leave the city buzz behind, head to nearby Red Rocks, the world's finest open-air amphitheatre, for a concert under the stars or a morning yoga session.

Colourful mural in the RiNo District

The Bluebird Theater music venue

Denver Art Museum

Train chugs along the rocky "Highline" ridge above the Animas River Valley

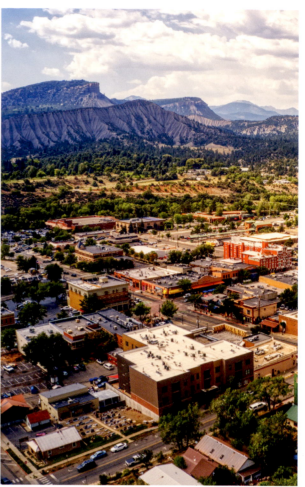

Durango

DURANGO & SILVERTON NARROW GAUGE RAILROAD

COLORADO The unforgettable Durango & Silverton Narrow Gauge Railroad corkscrews through spectacular scenery from Durango to the mining town of Silverton. Between May and October, steam trains make up to three daily return trips along a stunningly beautiful route through the mountains, clinging to the side of the Animas River canyon, at points 400ft above the river.

Trains depart from Durango, southwest Colorado's largest town. Founded in 1880 as a refining town and rail junction to serve Silverton 45 miles north, Durango enjoys a splendid setting amid the San Juan Mountains. A friendly, ebullient place, it's home these days to a mixed population of teleworkers and outdoor enthusiasts, who enjoy its year-round activities, excellent restaurants and flourishing arts scene.

The turnaround point for the railroad comes at Silverton: "silver by the ton", allegedly. Spread across a small flat valley and hemmed in entirely by tall mountain peaks, it's one of Colorado's most evocative (and secluded) mountain towns, where wide, dirt-paved streets lead off towards the surrounding heights. Although the false-fronted stores along "Notorious Blair Street" may remind one of the days when Wyatt Earp dealt cards here, the town is defined by the restaurants and gift shops that fill up around noon, when train passengers are in town.

Choo choo!

GLACIER NATIONAL PARK

MONTANA Two thousand lakes, a thousand miles of rivers, thick forests, breezy meadows and awe-inspiring peaks make up one of America's finest attractions, Glacier National Park – a haven for bighorn sheep, mountain goats, black and grizzly bears, wolves and mountain lions. Although the park does hold 25 small (and rapidly retreating) glaciers, it really takes its name from the huge flows of ice that carved these immense valleys twenty thousand years ago. In the summer months this is prime hiking and white-water rafting territory, while huckleberries litter the slopes in autumn.

The fifty-mile Going-to-the-Sun Road across the heart of the park is one of the most mesmerizing drives in the country, and driving it from west to east can take several hours – each successive hairpin brings a new colossus into view. Beginning at West Glacier, the road runs east along ten-mile Lake McDonald before starting to climb, as snowmelt from waterfalls gushes across the road, and the winding route nudges over the Continental Divide at Logan Pass (6680ft).

Bearhat Mountain and Hidden Lake

Bull moose in the autumn

Hiking in the park

View over Jackson Hole

A vibrant Teton thistle

GRAND TETON NATIONAL PARK

WYOMING The jagged tooth-like peaks of Grand Teton National Park are a magnificent spectacle, sheer-faced cliffs rising abruptly some 7000ft above the valley floor. A string of gem-like lakes is set tight at the foot of the mountains; the park also encompasses the broad, sagebrush-covered Jackson Hole river basin (a "hole" was a pioneer term for a flat, mountain-ringed valley), broken by the gently winding Snake River and home to elk, bison and moose.

At the heart of the park lies tranquil Jackson Lake, a glacial remnant rich in trout and mountain whitefish. From Colter Bay Visitor Center rented boats, canoes and kayaks cruise the calm, icy fresh waters, ringed by dense forests of spruce and fir. Elegant Jackson Lake Lodge sits right on the water offering awesome views, while Signal Mountain offers a breathtaking panorama of the lake and the Tetons beyond.

Canoeing on Jackson Lake

A'KAVEHE'ONAHE
LIMBER BONES
A CHEYENNE WARRIOR
FELL HERE ON
JUNE 25, 1876
WHILE DEFENDING
THE CHEYENNE
WAY OF LIFE

Native American headstone

Pathway around the site

7th Cavalry Memorial

Native American monument

A group of headstones, including Custer's

LITTLE BIGHORN BATTLEFIELD NATIONAL MONUMENT

MONTANA With the exception of Gettysburg (see page 25), no other US battle has gripped the American imagination like the Battle of the Little Bighorn in June 1876, the biggest defeat of US forces by Native Americans in the West and the scene of the much-mythologized "Custer's Last Stand". Once seen as a tragic hero, Custer is better known today for a series of blunders leading up to the battle, and the decisive Native American victory – of combined Arapaho, Lakota Sioux and Cheyenne warriors – helped shaped the legends of leaders Sitting Bull and Crazy Horse.

The battlefield is located on the current Crow Indian Reservation in the Little Bighorn Valley, and you can trace the course of the battle on a self-guided driving tour through the grasslands; there are also several hiking trails. What makes Little Bighorn so unique is that the landscape has remained virtually unchanged since 1876; equally unusual, white headstone markers show where each cavalryman was killed, while red granite markers do the same for Native American warriors, making for an extremely evocative experience. The visitor centre only contains a small exhibit on the battle, so to get the most out of the site listen to a ranger talk or take a free ranger tour.

The ladder to reach Long House

Petroglyphs at Mesa Verde National Park

Kivas, religious rooms, and a view of the canyon at Long House

Kiva ladder found in Spruce Tree House

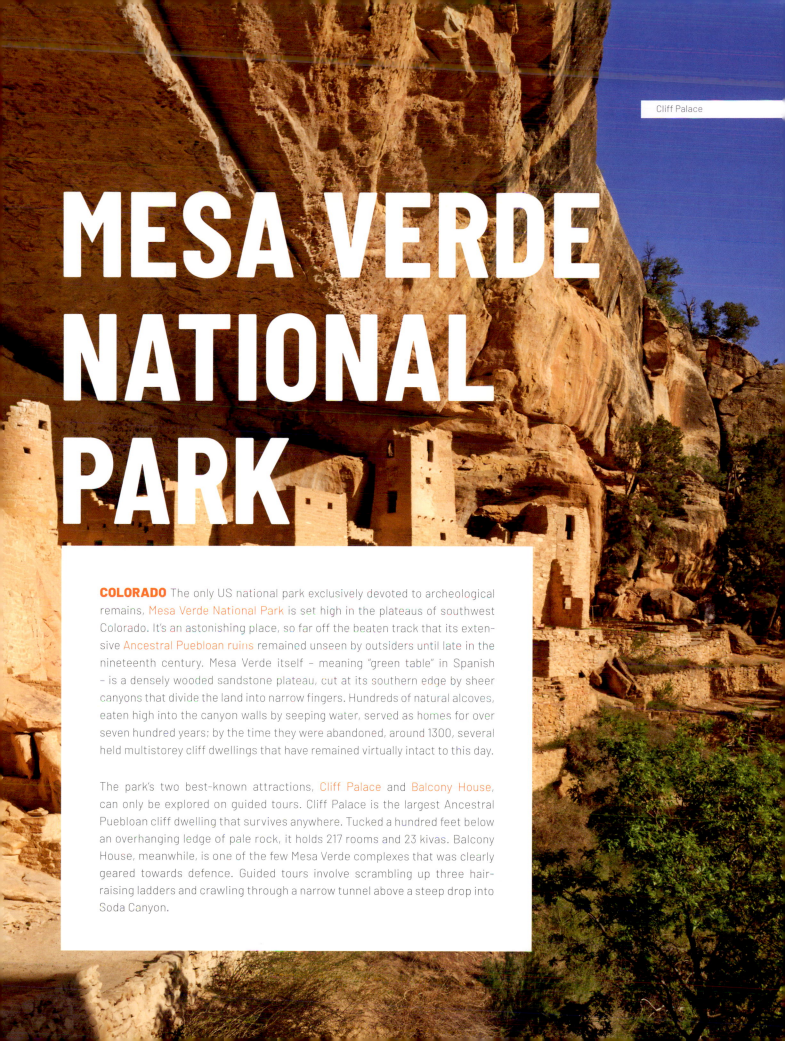

Cliff Palace

MESA VERDE NATIONAL PARK

COLORADO The only US national park exclusively devoted to archeological remains, Mesa Verde National Park is set high in the plateaus of southwest Colorado. It's an astonishing place, so far off the beaten track that its extensive Ancestral Puebloan ruins remained unseen by outsiders until late in the nineteenth century. Mesa Verde itself – meaning "green table" in Spanish – is a densely wooded sandstone plateau, cut at its southern edge by sheer canyons that divide the land into narrow fingers. Hundreds of natural alcoves, eaten high into the canyon walls by seeping water, served as homes for over seven hundred years; by the time they were abandoned, around 1300, several held multistorey cliff dwellings that have remained virtually intact to this day.

The park's two best-known attractions, Cliff Palace and Balcony House, can only be explored on guided tours. Cliff Palace is the largest Ancestral Puebloan cliff dwelling that survives anywhere. Tucked a hundred feet below an overhanging ledge of pale rock, it holds 217 rooms and 23 kivas. Balcony House, meanwhile, is one of the few Mesa Verde complexes that was clearly geared towards defence. Guided tours involve scrambling up three hair-raising ladders and crawling through a narrow tunnel above a steep drop into Soda Canyon.

Gem Lake in Rocky Mountain National Park

ROCKY MOUNTAINS

VARIOUS Only when you traverse the Rocky Mountain states of Colorado, Wyoming, Montana and Idaho does the immense size of the American West really hit home. Stretching for over one thousand miles from the virgin forests on the Canadian border to the deserts of New Mexico, America's rugged spine encompasses an astonishing array of landscapes – geyser basins, lava flows, arid valleys and huge sand dunes – each in its own way as dramatic as the region's magnificent snow-capped peaks. All that geological grandeur is enhanced by its glorious wildlife and the conspicuous legacy of the miners, cowboys, outlaws and Native Americans who struggled over the area's rich resources during the nineteenth century.

To experience the full, pristine grandeur of the Rockies, and especially its wildlife, a visit to the Rocky Mountain National Park in Colorado is essential. The park straddles the Continental Divide at elevations often well in excess of 10,000ft, with large sections inhabited by elk herds, moose, black bears and bighorn sheep. A full third of the park is above the tree line, and large areas of snow never melt; the name of the Never Summer Mountains speaks volumes about the long, empty expanses of arctic-style tundra. The park's lower reaches, among the rich forests, hold patches of lush greenery; you never know when you may stumble upon a sheltered mountain meadow flecked with flowers.

Indian paintbrush wildflowers line the steep mountainside on Bierstadt Moraine

Marmot in Rocky Mountain National Park

Alpine tundra on the Ute Crossing Trailhead

The Odessa Lake outlet below Little Matterhorn

View of the highway from Galena Summit

The long highway

Paddleboarding on Redfish Lake

Winter fly-fishing on the Salmon River

SAWTOOTH SCENIC BYWAY

IDAHO North of Ketchum and Sun Valley in central Idaho, Hwy-75 climbs through rising tracts of forest and mountains to top out after twenty miles at the spectacular panorama of Galena Summit (8701ft). Spreading out far below, the meadows of the Sawtooth Valley stretch northward. The winding road – dubbed the Sawtooth Scenic Byway – meanders beside the young Salmon River, whose headwaters rise in the forbidding icy peaks to the south, as the serrated ridge of the Sawtooth Mountains forms an impenetrable barrier along the western horizon. The main highlight along this stretch is Redfish Lake (just off the highway), beautifully framed by Mount Heyburn and Grand Mogul peaks, home to sockeye salmon and plenty of hiking and camping opportunities in the area of alpine lakes known as Shangri-La. Visit Redfish Center & Gallery by the lake for information, wildlife talks and boat trips.

The road to Galena Summit

The thrill of skiing in Telluride

Fun on the slopes

Main Street

Mountain Village in autumn

Bridal Veil Falls

TELLURIDE

COLORADO Set in a picturesque valley, at the flat base of vast steep-sided mountains, Telluride is a former mining village that was briefly home to the young Butch Cassidy, who robbed his first bank here in 1889. These days, it's better known as a top-class ski resort that rivals Aspen for celebrity allure. Happily, it has achieved its status without losing its character, exemplified by the beautifully preserved low-slung buildings along its wide main street. Healthy young bohemians with few visible means of support but top-notch ski equipment seem to form the bulk of the twelve hundred inhabitants, while most visitors tend to stay two miles up from town in Mountain Village, served by a free, year-round gondola service. Summer hiking opportunities are excellent; one three-mile round-trip walk leads from the head of the valley, where the highway ends at Pioneer Mill, up to the 431ft Bridal Veil Falls, the tallest in Colorado.

Herd of bison in Hayden Valley

YELLOWSTONE NATIONAL PARK

WYOMING America's oldest and easily its most famous national park, Yellowstone draws in the punters for good reason: the sheer diversity of what's on offer is mind-bending. Not only does Yellowstone deliver jaw-dropping mountain scenery, from the scintillating colours of the Grand Canyon of the Yellowstone to the deep-azure Yellowstone Lake and wild flower-filled meadows, but it's jam-packed with so much wildlife you might think you've arrived at a safari park. Shambling grizzly bears, vast herds of heavy-bearded bison and horned elk mingle with marmots, prairie dogs, eagles, coyotes and more than a dozen elusive wolf packs on the prowl.

What really sets Yellowstone apart, however, is that this is one of the world's largest volcanoes, with thermal activity providing half the world's geysers, thousands of fumaroles jetting plumes of steam, mud pots gurgling with acid-dissolved muds and clays, and, of course, hot springs. The park might not look like a volcano, but that's because the caldera is so big – 55km by 72km – and because, thankfully, it hasn't exploded for 640,000 years.

Yellowstone Lake

Great Fountain Geyser

Grizzly bear

Majestic bull elk

THE
PACIFIC
COAST

BIG SUR

CALIFORNIA The California coast doesn't get more astounding than Big Sur. With the rugged Santa Lucia Mountains on one side and craggy cliffs dropping into the Pacific Ocean to the other, this area is best viewed cruising along Route 1 – among the most exceptional drives in the country.

In an increasingly busy world, this ninety-or-so-mile stretch actively encourages you to slow down and breathe in the beauty. There's little wonder it's attracted artists of all varieties for generations, from the Beats to the hippies. But it's no good to stay cramped "ooh"-ing and "ahh"-ing from inside a car. Time must be made to get out and explore the bewitching coastline – often shrouded in a mesmerizing mist – and hike in its numerous parks. McWay Falls is so pictu-resque it's hard to believe you haven't simply willed it into existence, and the purple sand and serenity of Pfeiffer Beach is unrivalled.

For being such a household name in California, and one of the USA's ultimate road trips, Big Sur is surprisingly unspoilt. And even the developed areas are something special – one bite at *Nepenthe* restaurant, one glimpse of Bixby Bridge, and you'll be hooked.

View towards Bixby Bridge

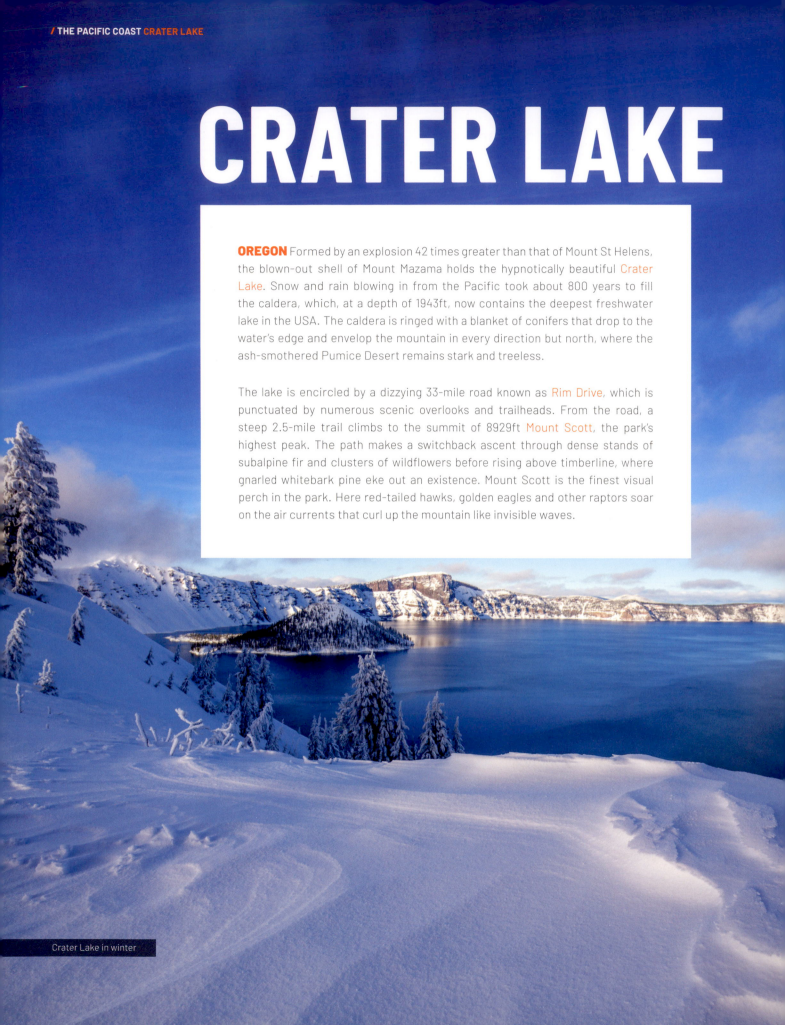

CRATER LAKE

OREGON Formed by an explosion 42 times greater than that of Mount St Helens, the blown-out shell of Mount Mazama holds the hypnotically beautiful Crater Lake. Snow and rain blowing in from the Pacific took about 800 years to fill the caldera, which, at a depth of 1943ft, now contains the deepest freshwater lake in the USA. The caldera is ringed with a blanket of conifers that drop to the water's edge and envelop the mountain in every direction but north, where the ash-smothered Pumice Desert remains stark and treeless.

The lake is encircled by a dizzying 33-mile road known as Rim Drive, which is punctuated by numerous scenic overlooks and trailheads. From the road, a steep 2.5-mile trail climbs to the summit of 8929ft Mount Scott, the park's highest peak. The path makes a switchback ascent through dense stands of subalpine fir and clusters of wildflowers before rising above timberline, where gnarled whitebark pine eke out an existence. Mount Scott is the finest visual perch in the park. Here red-tailed hawks, golden eagles and other raptors soar on the air currents that curl up the mountain like invisible waves.

Crater Lake in winter

Hiker overlooking Crater Lake from Mount Scott

Whitebark pine on the West Rim

Bike trail at Mazama Campground

Kīlauea erupting

HAWAI'I VOLCANOES NATIONAL PARK

HAWAI'I A sweet smell lingers in the air at Hawai'i Volcanoes National Park, no matter the time of year. Its harbingers are the wildflowers that carpet the park's fertile lava fields, masking the faintly sulphuric tangs and bringing colour to this dark, lunar landscape. Jungles also abound, surrounding the crater rim of vast Kīlauea, one of the world's largest volcanoes, threatening to wipe out the vegetation with a fresh flow of molten lava. Steam vents interrupt the terrain: deep holes where vivid green epiphytes grow in the cracks of the jagged brown rock and vapour escapes the earth. In this land of steam and fire, visitors can walk across an active lava field, see the glow of molten rock as it rises and bubbles from the volcanoes, and drive along Chain of Craters Road all the way to the coast, where the lava has been stopped in its tracks and turned to black rock.

Pu'u Loa petroglyphs carved into hardened lava

Lava tube

Jungle trail

Molten lava flowing into the Pacific Ocean on Big Island

Red Dog Saloon on Franklin Street

St Nicholas Russian Orthodox Church

Juneau Harbor with a sea plane

Hikers on the glacier

JUNEAU

ALASKA The sheer size of Alaska is hard to grasp. Superimposed on to the Lower 48 states, it would stretch from the Atlantic to the Pacific, while its coastline is longer than that of the rest of the mainland USA combined. Its state capital, the sophisticated and vibrant city of Juneau, is the only in the nation not accessible by road.

Juneau is exceptionally picturesque, wedged between the Gastineau Channel and the rainforested hills behind. In 1880, Joe Juneau made Alaska's first gold strike here, and until the last mine closed in 1944 this was the world's largest producer of low-grade ore. Many original buildings stand in the South Franklin Street Historic District – Juneau managed to avoid the fires that destroyed many other gold towns in Alaska. The onion-domed St Nicholas Russian Orthodox Church contains icons and religious treasures, while the well-presented Alaska State Museum covers Native culture, Russian heritage and the first gold strikes. The city's draws are capped by the drive-to Mendenhall Glacier and the watery charms of Tracy Arm fjord.

Ice climbing on the Mendenhall Glacier

Nā Pali Coast

Waipo'o Falls, Waimea Canyon

Hanalei Bay

Be prepared on the Kalalau Trial

Lush vegetation in the Nā Pali Coast State Park

KAUAI

HAWAI'I Lush rainforests, colossal canyons, cascading waterfalls and emerald valleys – the Hawaiian island of Kauai, the oldest of the archipelago, is arrestingly beautiful. Known as the "Garden Isle" and still largely undeveloped, Kauai offers travellers breathtaking back-to-nature experiences in pristine tropical surrounds.

On the west of the island, Waimea Canyon State Park is blessed with 45 miles of trails, lacing their way across striking red-rock cliffs, as well as the epic Waipo'o Falls. Nicknamed the Grand Canyon of the Pacific, the canyon itself spans a ten-mile-long crater that drops to a depth of 3600ft. Further north, the eleven-mile Kalalau Trail within the Nā Pali Coast State Park (familiar from films such as *Jurassic Park* and *South Pacific*) is oft cited as one of the world's most spectacular – and dangerous – hiking routes. Beginning at show-stopping, reef-protected Ke'e Beach before criss-crossing streams and jungle terrain, as well as taking in secret sea caves and the cathedral-like Hanakoa Falls, this trail offers experienced hikers an exhilarating challenge.

While Kauai's landscapes are irrefutably wild, the island has a charmingly chilled vibe. Backed by majestic mountains, the crescent-shaped bay in quaint Hanalei Town on the north shore is the perfect spot to unwind.

North Shore of Lake Tahoe Secret Harbor

South Lake Tahoe in winter

Kayaking on the lake

Zephyr Cove beach

Snowboarding in the mountains above the lake

LAKE TAHOE

CALIFORNIA One of the highest, deepest, cleanest and coldest lakes in the world, Lake Tahoe is perched high above the Gold Country in an alpine bowl of forested granite peaks. Longer than the English Channel is wide, and more than 1000ft deep, it's so cold that perfectly preserved cowboys who drowned more than a century ago have been recovered from its depths. The lake straddles the Nevada state line as well and lures weekenders with sunny beaches in the summer, snow-covered slopes in the winter and bustling casinos year-round.

In South Lake Tahoe, the lakeside's largest community, ranks of restaurants, modest motels and pine-bound cottages stand cheek by jowl with the high-rise gambling dens of Stateline, just across the border in Nevada. If you happen to lose your money at the table and slot machines, you can always explore the beautiful hiking trails, parks and beaches in the surrounding area. Tahoe City, meanwhile, the hub on the lake's northwestern shore, manages to retain a more relaxed small-town attitude. And for those in search of some thrilling winter sports, the region rivals the Rocky Mountains in offering some of the best downhill skiing and snowboarding in North America.

Flowers in Downtown Los Angeles

Funky mural in the Arts District

Lifeguard tower on Venice Beach

The Los Angeles skyline

LOS ANGELES

CALIFORNIA Lights, camera, Los Angeles! This sprawling, sun-dappled metropolis is stepping into the spotlight in the new decade with an impressive array of cultural projects, expanded neighbourhoods and daring restaurants.

In late 2021, Los Angeles is unveiling a stunning new museum dedicated to its most famous export: cinema. The Academy Museum of Motion Pictures, designed by Renzo Piano, is one of the world's largest museums focused on the art and science of the movies. An architectural and artistic renaissance is also energizing Downtown Los Angeles (DTLA), among the fastest-growing urban neighbourhoods in the United States. DTLA's flourishing Arts District is an epicentre for contemporary art, and the cultural corridor of Grand Avenue is helmed by the swooping Frank Gehry-designed Walt Disney Concert Hall, home to the L.A. Philharmonic. The neighbourhood's shops and restaurants are equally dynamic, from designer boutiques featuring "made in L.A." fashions to restaurants that celebrate global cuisines. Best of all? DTLA is one of the few L.A. neighbourhoods that's largely pedestrianized – and well-connected to the rest of the city by metro – so you can explore without getting snarled in traffic. But in the end, the grand enticement of Los Angeles is its proximity to the sea, and the coast is dotted with palm-fringed communities, including Santa Monica, Venice and Hermosa Beach, where you can frolic on the beach, and then toast the evening at an outdoor bar strung with fairy lights.

OLYMPIC NATIONAL PARK

WASHINGTON Magnificent Olympic National Park, comprising the colossal Olympic Mountains in the heart of the Olympic Peninsula plus a separate, isolated sixty-mile strip of Pacific coastline further west, is one of Washington's prime wilderness destinations. It features raging rivers, alpine meadows, sizeable tracts of moss-draped rainforest and boundless opportunities for spectacular hiking and wildlife watching. Black-tailed deer are fairly common and quite relaxed around people wielding cameras; black bears, Roosevelt elk and cougars are rarer to spot.

Around 95 percent of the park is designated wilderness and inaccessible by car; no roads go through the middle but instead enter the interior from its edge like spokes on a wheel. The main visitor centre stands in Port Angeles, where a 17-mile scenic road winds its way up to Hurricane Ridge. At 5242ft, this affords mesmerizing views of the jagged peaks around Mount Olympus itself, clothed in the pearly white robe of Blue Glacier and at 7980ft, the park's highest point (its peak only accessible to professional mountaineers). Seven glaciers hang from Olympus; its massive shoulders have been draped in ice for thousands of years, though its glaciers continue to decrease in size.

Hoh Rainforest

Lake Crescent, Olympic National Park

Sol Duc Falls

Bainbridge Island ferry dock

Mid-century architecture

Glitz and glamour at Palm Springs Pride

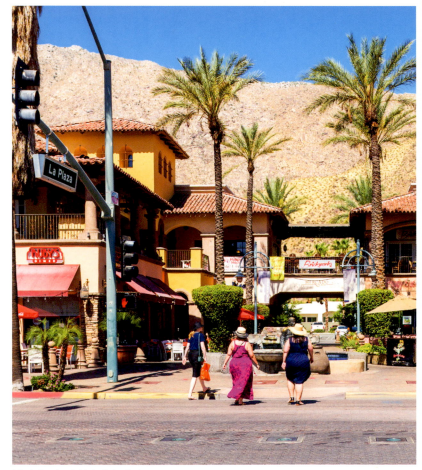

Life is lived outside in Palm Springs

Hiking in Mount San Jacinto State Park

The Joshua tree is found only in the Mojave Desert

PALM SPRINGS AND JOSHUA TREE

CALIFORNIA Popularized in the 1950s by studio-owned movie stars whose contracts kept them within two hours of Hollywood, showbiz glamour still flows effortlessly around the delightful small city of Palm Springs. Progressive architects and forward-thinking designers created cutting-edge modernist homes and offices, leaving a unique collection of dynamic mid-twentieth century buildings. The climate is perfect for outdoor living almost year-round, with open-air concerts, alfresco dining, cycling, trail hiking and almost every recreation activity ever invented. Glimpses of snow-covered mountains, framed by clear blue skies, are visible through the palm trees on a winter's day. Mount San Jacinto State Park can be reached by cable car, giving stunning views along the entire Coachella Valley. Across the valley, meanwhile, is Joshua Tree National Park, a vast protected area of pristine desert, weathered granite rock formations and abandoned gold mines. The area's pioneering spirit continues today – pretty much anything goes in this laidback LGBTQ-friendly Californian hotspot.

Beach in Redwood National Park

Roosevelt elk

Gold Bluffs campgrounds in Redwood National Park

Redwoods and coastal fog

REDWOOD NATIONAL PARK

CALIFORNIA Enormous, ancient redwoods are the star attractions at Redwood National Park, established in 1968 to protect Northern California's forests from logging. Here, one of the few remaining groves of coastal redwood, sequoia sempervirens, grows just a few minutes' walk from the relentlessly pounding surf of the Pacific Ocean. The giants rise prodigiously, some to a height of more than 300ft. Roosevelt elk graze on roadside prairies, salmon and trout swim in streams and rivers, and a wide range of birdlife inhabits the shore and forest. Besides its trees, Redwood's other spectacular attribute, the nearly 40-miles of rugged Pacific Coast where seals and sea lions splash in the waves, is accessible to hikers via the Coastal Trail.

Sunrise in the park

Salvation Mountain mailbox

Salvation Mountain

Welcome sign

East Jesus art

Entrance sign to Slab City

SALVATION MOUNTAIN

CALIFORNIA With its optimistic spirit and a climate that lends itself to laidback bohemianism, Southern California has long attracted artists and eccentrics. One place where this free-spirited energy soars is Salvation Mountain, and its nearby off-grid community. A startling sight in the scorching desert, between the Salton Sea and the Chocolate Mountains, this psychedelic masterpiece is the life's work of the late Leonard Knight. Over 28 years,

he crafted his folk-art complex from clay, hay and half a million gallons of latex paint. At five storeys high and 150ft wide, its giant crowning slogan "God Is Love" spreads an offering of warmth in this hostile environment.

Salvation Mountain is a fitting monument at the entrance to Slab City. Almost featureless on a map, this square-mile former Marine training facility is now one of the country's largest vehicle squats, the community of RVs and trailers hailed as the "Last Free Place". Capturing this sprit is their steampunk-inspired sculpture garden, East Jesus, where the self-sufficient residents rebirth junk as art. According to them, whether a visitor drops by for a picture, or stays in the hope of a spiritual awakening, no one leaves unchanged.

Alcatraz

Golden Gate Bridge

Victorian houses located near scenic Alamo Square

Chinatown

SAN FRANCISCO

CALIFORNIA One of the USA's most stunningly sited cities, San Francisco sits poised on the northern tip of a slender peninsula along the California coast. Home of the Golden Gate Bridge, Alcatraz, hippies, Levi's and Craigslist, it's arguably the most beautiful, and probably the most progressive major city in the country: an individualistic place whose residents pride themselves on living in a city like few – if any – in the world. It's a surprisingly compact and approachable place, broken up by 43 windswept hills, where downtown streets rise on impossible gradients to reveal stunning views, and where fog rolls in on a moment's notice to envelop everything in a mist.

Tucked on and around the hills of San Francisco are dozens of small, distinct neighbourhoods with their own character, microclimates and special attractions. Landmarks like Chinatown, Alcatraz and the city's cable cars, as well as lesser-known attractions – mural-lined alleys, a literary festival and a 1910 hardware store that sells just about everything – all contribute to the special charm of the City by the Bay.

Sunset over Natural Bridges State Park

SANTA CRUZ

CALIFORNIA Outdoor adventuring isn't just a pastime in Santa Cruz, it's a way of life. This eco-pioneer on California's sun-baked central coast continues to lead the way in embracing nature. A new wave of hike and bike trails snake along the sea, showcasing the glories of Santa Cruz, from isolated coves to frothy waves bobbing with surfers. Santa Cruz County abounds in flourishing parkland, including Natural Bridges State Park on the salty edges of the Pacific, famed for its soaring stone arch. Peer under the sea at tide pools wriggling with aquatic creatures, or look to the skies for migrating monarch butterflies in autumn and winter. The Santa Cruz Mountains sprout magnificent redwoods – some mighty elders are more than 2000 years old – in the Henry Cowell Redwoods State Park. Stroll the hushed, magical grove of old-growth redwoods, and then splash into the Garden of Eden swimming hole. Beyond the natural riches is the retro allure of the Santa Cruz Beach Boardwalk – bright with amusement-park rides and casino arcades – and a new influx of craft breweries across the region, where you can sample unique beers scented with local berries.

Santa Cruz Beach Boardwalk

Santa Cruz Yacht Club

Colourful houses in the California sun

SEATTLE

WASHINGTON Think Seattle, think rock. Endless musical legends have emerged from the largest city in Washington state: rock royalty such as Pearl Jam, Soundgarden and Alice In Chains all hail from here – and no-one can forget the grunge geniuses that were Nirvana. Music resonates throughout the entire city, with its exciting melange of venues, and a thrilling number of festivals are held here, such as the multigenre Bumbershoot and the alternative Northwest Folkfire Festival. And while the Museum of Pop Culture (MoPOP) is crammed with musical artefacts, including the largest collection of Jimi Hendrix memorabilia in the world, Seattle is also a creative hotbed for other arts. At the remarkable Chihuly Garden and Glass Museum you can admire twinkling glass creations in the shapes of towering bushes and spindly trees, while the sparkling glasshouse has delicate blooming flowers suspended from its roof. Watch the fiery red reflections dance off the surfaces, while the soothing ambers gently warm the space – it's a spellbinding riot of colour.

Bumbershoot festival

The Wrangell Mountains

WRANGELL-
ST ELIAS
NATIONAL PARK

ALASKA A wild and magnificent alpine world, Wrangell-St Elias National Park is – at 20625 square miles – bigger than Switzerland and by far the country's largest national park. Within its boundaries lie four major mountain ranges and six of the continent's ten highest peaks, including 18008ft Mount St Elias, as well as the Wrangell Volcanic Field. Made up of thousands of lava flows and towering craters, the latter includes Mount Wrangell, one of the largest active volcanoes (by volume) in the world and the only one active in the Wrangell Mountains – steam plumes often rise from its summit.

Here, too, is North America's largest subpolar icefield, the Bagley, which feeds a system of gigantic glaciers, including the Tana, Miles and Guyot. Rock walls rise thousands of feet above glacially carved canyons, while rugged, remote coastline is bounded by tidewater glaciers and jagged peaks.

One of the park's best-known overland routes, the primitive and rugged Goat Trail was traditionally used by Athabaskan people for hunting and trading. Even today, a diverse range of wildlife call this wintry habitat home, including Dall sheep, moose, bears, mountain goats, caribou and even two herds of transplanted bison.

The Kennicott Glacier

Hiking the extinct Skookum Volcano

Mount Drum over the Copper River

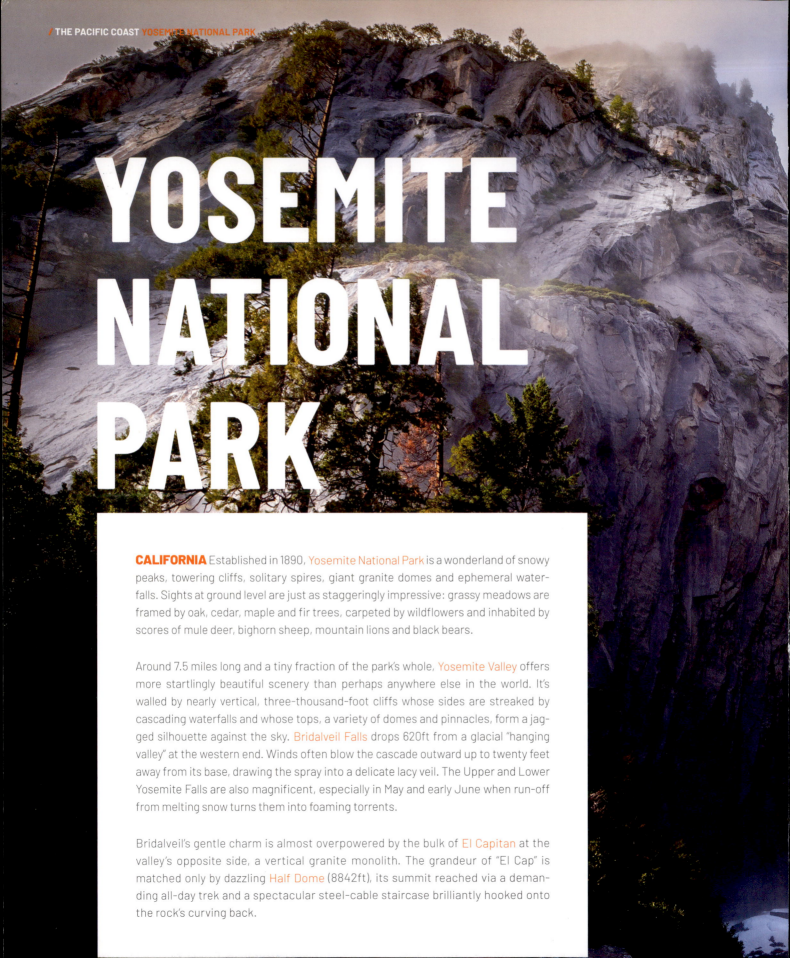

YOSEMITE NATIONAL PARK

CALIFORNIA Established in 1890, Yosemite National Park is a wonderland of snowy peaks, towering cliffs, solitary spires, giant granite domes and ephemeral water-falls. Sights at ground level are just as staggeringly impressive: grassy meadows are framed by oak, cedar, maple and fir trees, carpeted by wildflowers and inhabited by scores of mule deer, bighorn sheep, mountain lions and black bears.

Around 7.5 miles long and a tiny fraction of the park's whole, Yosemite Valley offers more startlingly beautiful scenery than perhaps anywhere else in the world. It's walled by nearly vertical, three-thousand-foot cliffs whose sides are streaked by cascading waterfalls and whose tops, a variety of domes and pinnacles, form a jagged silhouette against the sky. Bridalveil Falls drops 620ft from a glacial "hanging valley" at the western end. Winds often blow the cascade outward up to twenty feet away from its base, drawing the spray into a delicate lacy veil. The Upper and Lower Yosemite Falls are also magnificent, especially in May and early June when run-off from melting snow turns them into foaming torrents.

Bridalveil's gentle charm is almost overpowered by the bulk of El Capitan at the valley's opposite side, a vertical granite monolith. The grandeur of "El Cap" is matched only by dazzling Half Dome (8842ft), its summit reached via a demanding all-day trek and a spectacular steel-cable staircase brilliantly hooked onto the rock's curving back.

Yosemite Falls

INDEX

CONTRIBUTORS

Jacqui Agate

Susie Boulton

Chris Bradley

Jenny Cahill-Jones

Nick Edwards

Stephen Keeling

Rachel Lawrence

Nicky Leach

Joe Legate

Sîan Marsh

Rachel Mills

Joanne Owen

Kirsten Powley

Robert Savage

Zara Sekhavati

AnneLise Sorensen

Paul Stafford

Jamie Tabberer

Greg Ward

Annie Warren

Siobhan Warwicker

Aimée White

PHOTO CREDITS

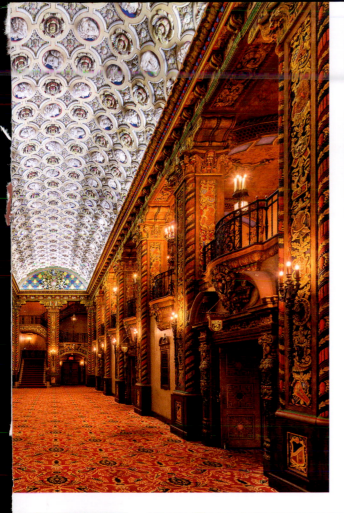